Backroad Bicycling in New Hampshire

A historic church in Kensington

Backroad Bicycling in
New Hampshire

ANDI MARIE CANTELE

32 Scenic Rides
Along Country Lanes
in the Granite State

Backcountry Guides
Woodstock, Vermont

AN INVITATION TO THE READER   Although it is unlikely that
the roads you cycle on these tours will change much with time, some road
signs, landmarks, and other items may. If you find that such changes have
occurred on these routes, please let the author and publisher know, so that cor-
rections may be made in future editions. Other comments and suggestions are
also welcome. Address all correspondence to: Editor, Backroad Bicycling Series,
Backcountry Guides, P.O. Box 748, Woodstock, VT 05091.

Copyright © 2004 by Andi Marie Cantele

First Edition

Library of Congress Cataloging-in-Publication Data
Cantele, Andi Marie, 1969–
  Backroad bicycling in New Hampshire : 32 scenic rides along country lanes in
the Granite State / Andi Marie Cantele. —1st ed.
    p. cm.
  ISBN 0-88150-610-9
  1. Bicycle touring—New Hampshire—Guidebooks. 2. New Hampshire—
Guidebooks. I. Title.
GV1045.5.N4C36 2004
796.6'4'09742—dc22

                                2004043768

Cover and interior design by Bodenweber Design
Composition by PerfecType, Nashville, TN
Cover photograph © David Brownell
Maps by Moore Creative Designs, © 2004 The Countryman Press

Published by Backcountry Guides, an imprint of The Countryman Press, P.O.
Box 748, Woodstock, Vermont 05091

Distributed by W. W. Norton & Company, Inc., 500 Fifth Avenue, New York, NY
10110

Printed in the United States of America

10 9 8 7 6 5 4 3 2 1

For Brian

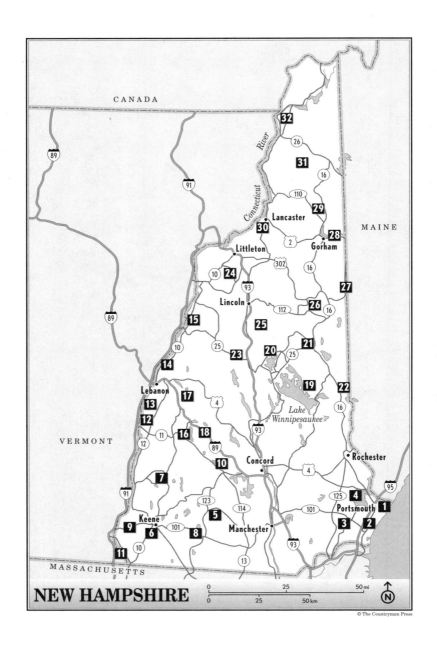

CANADA

MAINE

VERMONT

MASSACHUSETTS

Lancaster

Littleton

Lincoln

Lebanon

Keene

Concord

Manchester

Rochester

Portsmouth

Lake
Winnipesaukee

Connecticut River

Gorham

NEW HAMPSHIRE

0   25   50 mi
0   25   50 km

© The Countryman Press

CONTENTS

9   Acknowledgments

10   Backroad Bicycle Tours at a Glance

15   Introduction

SOUTHERN NEW HAMPSHIRE: THE SEACOAST TO THE MONADNOCKS

27   **1** Portsmouth to New Castle

33   **2** The Atlantic Seacoast Tour

37   **3** Exeter

43   **4** The Great Bay via Durham and Newmarket

47   **5** Hill Villages: Bennington, Francestown, Greenfield

53   **6** Swanzey Covered Bridges

57   **7** Western Monadnock Villages

61   **8** Peterborough

67   **9** Spofford Lake via Westmoreland and Chesterfield

71   **10** Bradford, Henniker, Warner: A Monadnock/Merrimack Tour

THE CONNECTICUT RIVER VALLEY

79   **11** New Hampshire–Massachusetts–Vermont: A Three-State Tour

85   **12** Windsor, Vermont, via the Cornish-Windsor Covered Bridge

89   **13** The Cornish Colony

95   **14** Dartmouth College

99   **15** River Villages

THE LAKES REGION

107   **16** Lake Sunapee

111 **17** Enfield Shaker Village
117 **18** Colby-Sawyer College
121 **19** Lake Winnipesaukee
127 **20** Squam Lake
133 **21** Tamworth and Ossipee
137 **22** The Wakefield Lakes

THE WHITE MOUNTAINS
145 **23** The Baker River Valley
149 **24** Sugar Hill
155 **25** Tripoli Road
159 **26** The Kancamagus Highway via Bear Notch
165 **27** Border Tour: New Hampshire and Maine

THE GREAT NORTH WOODS
171 **28** The Androscoggin River
175 **29** Berlin to Milan
181 **30** Mount Orne Covered Bridge Ramble
185 **31** The Great North Woods Tour
191 **32** Northern River Roads: Colebrook to Pittsburg

ACKNOWLEDGMENTS Writing this book was possible thanks to the expertise, ideas, and support of many people whom I would like to recognize.

Bike shops across the state were generous with their knowledge and route ideas, especially Mike Micucci at Moriah Sports in Gorham; Mike Farrell at Durham Bike in Durham; John Gromek, Erik Froburg, and Dan Mattson at Exeter Cycles in Exeter; Charlie Southgate at Banagan's Cycling Company in Keene; Will Hurley at Outspokin' Bicycle and Sport in Newbury; Dave Harkless at Littleton Bike Shop in Littleton; Jonah Fernald at Portsmouth Rent & Ride; and the staffs at Rhino Bike Works in Plymouth, Red Jersey Cyclery in Bartlett, and Joe Jones Ski and Sport in North Conway.

I am also grateful to Dave Topham at Granite State Wheelmen, Beth Donald and George Gavutis of the Bicycle Coalition of New Hampshire, and Cameron Wake of Seacoast Area Bicycle Routes for sharing their local knowledge.

Thanks to Jean and Andy Fusco, Wayne and Janet Waldron, Felicia Jarosz, Suzette and Mark Andrade, and Jen Poll; thanks also to Barbara Dougeneck for her help on routes in the Monadnock Region, and Bill Houle for assistance on Ride 26: The Kancamagus Highway via Bear Notch.

Finally, I am grateful to Kermit Hummel, Jennifer Thompson, Darren Brown, Fred Lee, Kelly Thompson, and David Corey at Backcountry Guides for their guidance and expertise.

All of you helped make this book possible.

BACKROAD BICYCLE TOURS AT A GLANCE

RIDE	REGION	DISTA
1. Portsmouth to New Castle	Southern NH	14.3 m
2. The Atlantic Seacoast Tour	Southern NH	30 mil
3. Exeter	Southern NH	14.2 m
4. The Great Bay via Durham and Newmarket	Southern NH	17.7 m
5. Hill Villages: Bennington, Francestown, Greenfield	Southern NH	27 mil
6. Swanzey Covered Bridges	Southern NH	13.5 m
7. Western Monadnock Villages	Southern NH	31.6 m
8. Peterborough	Southern NH	28.6 m
9. Spofford Lake via Westmoreland and Chesterfield	Southern N H	23.5 m
10. Bradford, Henniker, Warner: A Monadnock/Merrimack Tour	Southern N H	34.4 m
11. New Hampshire–Massachusetts–Vermont: A Three-State Tour	River Valley	76.7 m
12. Windsor, Vermont, via the Cornish-Windsor Covered Bridge	River Valley	11.3 m
13. The Cornish Colony	River Valley	23 mil
14. Dartmouth College	River Valley	31 mil
15. River Villages	River Valley	41.1 m
16. Lake Sunapee	Lakes Region	20.5 m
17. Enfield Shaker Village	Lakes Region	40.7 m

DIFFICULTY	BIKE	KIDS?	HIGHLIGHTS
Easy	Road	Yes	A picturesque seacoast loop
Moderate	Road	No	A scenic stretch along the Atlantic Ocean
Easy to Moderate	Road	Yes	Rural roads on the outskirts of historic Exeter
Moderate	Road	No	Panoramic views of Great Bay
Strenuous	Hybrid	No	A trio of historic hill villages
Easy	Road	Yes	Four covered bridge crossings
Strenuous	Road	No	Quaint rural villages in the Monadnock Range
Strenuous	Road	No	New Hampshire's highest village center
Moderate to Strenuous	Road	No	Rural countryside and a pretty lake
Moderate to Strenuous	Road	No	The country's oldest railroad covered bridge
Very Strenuous	Road	No	Rural farmland along the Connecticut River
Easy	Road	Yes	The longest covered bridge in the United States
Moderate	Road	No	A rural 20th-century artists' colony
Moderate	Road	No	An Ivy League campus on the Connecticut River
Moderate to Strenuous	Road	No	Historic homes and picturesque farmland
Moderate to	Road	No	A pleasant loop around a scenic lake
Strenuous	Road	No	A preserved 18th-century Shaker village

RIDE	REGION	DISTA
18. Colby-Sawyer College	Lakes Region	29.2 m
19. Lake Winnipesaukee	Lakes Region	30 mil
20. Squam Lake	Lakes Region	27.4 m
21. Tamworth and Ossipee	Lakes Region	34 mil
22. The Wakefield Lakes	Lakes Region	40.2 m
23. The Baker River Valley	White Mountains	32.2 m
24. Sugar Hill	White Mountains	23.3 m
25. Tripoli Road	White Mountains	32.5 m
26. The Kancamagus Highway via Bear Notch	White Mountains	37.4 m
27. Border Tour: New Hampshire and Maine	White Mountains	40.5 m
28. The Androscoggin River	Great North Woods	24.8 m
29. Berlin to Milan	Great North Woods	27.9 m
30. Mount Orne Covered Bridge Ramble	Great North Woods	11.1 m
31. The Great North Woods Tour	Great North Woods	82.8 m
32. Northern River Roads: Colebrook to Pittsburg	Great North Woods	39.7 m

DIFFICULTY	BIKE	KIDS?	HIGHLIGHTS
Moderate to Strenuous	Road	No	A classic New England college town
Strenuous	Road	No	Rural villages and farmland along the western shoreline
Strenuous	Road	No	Ride past film locations from On Golden Pond
Moderate	Road	No	Wooded hills studded with lakes and ponds
Moderate to Strenuous	Road	No	A scenic tour along the rural Maine border
Moderate to Strenuous	Road	No	A scenic stretch of the Baker River
Strenuous	Road	No	A hilltop Colonial village with panoramic views
Strenuous	Hybrid	No	A challenging tour through Waterville Valley
Strenuous	Road	No	Bear Notch; Kancamagus Scenic Byway
Moderate to Strenuous	Road	No	Hidden villages along the Maine border
Easy to Moderate	Road	Yes	A meandering country road along the Androscoggin River
Strenuous	Road	No	A working mill town in New Hampshire's northern forest
Easy	Road	Yes	A covered bridge built in the early 1900s
Very Strenuous	Road	No	A challenging tour through the North Country
Strenuous	Road	No	The source of New England's longest river

INTRODUCTION For centuries, hordes of pioneers—and later tourists—have made their way to New Hampshire, lured by stories of natural wonders: craggy mountain peaks, sparkling lakes and rivers, and pristine forests rich in wildlife and timber. Impressed by the scenery, many settled for good, or at least returned year after year.

Today, the Granite State beckons cyclists of every persuasion with a landscape as diverse and beautiful as any in New England. Close to 85 percent of the state—about 4.5 million acres—is blanketed in forest. Verdant, gently sloping farmland stretches along the Connecticut River, while rocky coastline cuts a dramatic swath along the Atlantic Ocean. A wide scattering of cobalt lakes shimmer in the central hills, and a vast semiwilderness covers the state's northernmost tip. And while rambling stone walls crisscross the meadows and woods surrounding prim Colonial villages, the green hills and ridges of the Monadnocks march northward to the White Mountains' wild and Presidential Range—the highest peaks in the Northeast—and the rugged North Country uplands beyond.

This is a long state—roughly 200 miles north to south—which varies in width from a mere few miles along the Canadian border to nearly 100 miles along the Massachusetts state line in southern New Hampshire. There are more than 1,000 miles of state-designated scenic and cultural byways, not to mention the sprawling web of lightly traveled dirt roads and old-time country lanes. As a result, the bike routes reflect a fascinating diversity, from flat coastal areas to challenging mountainous terrain. Many rides pass by some of the state's 1,300 lakes and ponds, and others follow the courses of New Hampshire's 40-odd rivers, which total about 42,000 miles in length. Even the most heavily touristed areas have a number of hidden corners that are perfect for cycling.

I've divided the state into five regions: southern New Hampshire, from the seacoast to the wooded Monadnock Range; the Connecticut River valley, a fertile farming valley that extends from Quebec to Massachusetts; the central Lakes Region stretching from Lake Sunapee to the Maine border; the White Mountains, with the Northeast's largest national forest brimming with rugged granite peaks, twisting rivers, and hidden roads; and the Great North Woods, the state's notoriously desolate and wildly beautiful northernmost reaches. Each region has its own unique topography, history, and flavor.

Southern New Hampshire has four distinct parts: the stunning-yet-diminutive seacoast; the broad Merrimack Valley, with its bustling population and industrial centers in Concord, Manchester, and Nashua; the high and hilly Monadnock region,

A picturesque harbor on the Atlantic seacoast outside of Portsmouth

with its storybook villages; and the rural farming plain fed by the
Connecticut River. With their white, steepled churches and vintage meetinghouses, 18th- and 19th-century towns like Dublin,
Francestown, and Jaffrey Center look much as they did when
settled centuries ago, reminiscent of Norman Rockwell's images of
quintessential New England. The best ones must be sought out,
and tours often pass right by them.

New Hampshire supports more than three thousand commercial farms statewide, from dairies and sheep farms to apple
orchards and sugarhouses. Many are spread across the loamy
flood plains of the Connecticut River valley, a patchwork of cornfields, pastures, and meadows dotted with silos, rambling farmhouses, produce stands, and neat red barns. Historic river towns
like Orford and Haverhill, whose elegant architecture reflects the
prosperity on which they were founded centuries ago, are connected by rolling bucolic hills, making this long pastoral valley
along New England's mightiest river a cycling mecca. One of New
Hampshire's lesser-known nicknames is "Mother of Rivers," a nod
to the Connecticut and several other rivers that originate in the
state's mountains.

New Hampshire's midsection, known as the Lakes Region, is
dotted with hundreds of shimmering lakes and ponds that total
almost 200,000 acres of water, from the colossal Lake
Winnipesaukee to the more demure Squam Lake, with many
smaller but equally scenic ponds scattered between. The area
includes a picturesque mix of wooded hills, meandering country
lanes, and classic villages complete with general stores, grassy
commons, and rambling clapboard inns.

The White Mountains and Great North Woods offer the most
challenging terrain—lung-searing climbs and screaming descents,
with a stunning backdrop of New England's loftiest peaks. Visitors
from around the world come here for the fresh mountain air and
expansive views, or to climb 6,299-foot Mount Washington, the
highest peak east of the Rockies and north of the Mason-Dixon
Line. However, tucked inside the rugged landscape are pockets of
gentle terrain, thickly studded with farm fields and vintage barns
and the occasional Colonial village remarkably untouched by

progress. Reaching them by bike is often a challenge, but most cyclists agree that finding these enclaves is time and effort well spent.

Two of New Hampshire's most indelible images are its soaring mountains and blazing autumn foliage, both of which draw millions of visitors annually. A lesser-known but equally impressive icon is its stunning collection of some 64 vintage covered bridges, which span rivers and streams all over the state. Many of these tours pass over or near them.

A few of these historic bridges cross the Connecticut River, a prominent fixture in New Hampshire's geography and history. Indeed, the mighty river begins its long, slow course to Long Island Sound as a mere trickle in the state's uppermost reaches in Pittsburg, just shy of the Canadian border. It also serves as the state's 255-mile western border with Vermont. The Cornish-Windsor Covered Bridge, a 19th-century gem spanning the river between Cornish, New Hampshire, and Windsor, Vermont, is believed to be the longest covered bridge in the United States. And in the Merrimack Valley, the Hopkinton Bridge over the Contoocook River is said to be the country's oldest railroad covered bridge.

Historic sites are scattered throughout the state, from homes built when New Hampshire was one of the original 13 colonies to roadside memorials honoring the contributions of noteworthy local residents. Many local historical societies operate museums or host tours of preserved buildings, and more than 175 historic markers point out the Granite State's most important places.

New Hampshire's population of 1.3 million is concentrated in the southern and central parts of the state, leaving the rest blissfully serene. A network of scenic back roads winds through farmland and wooded hills, along rivers and coastal marshes, connecting centuries-old villages and strings of picturesque lakes. Collectively, they are an adventurous cyclist's dream, available to anyone willing to venture off the beaten path and explore them.

ABOUT THE RIDES   This book is your guide to all kinds of rides across New Hampshire. These routes were chosen for their natu-

Cornfields lining the banks of the Connecticut River in Orford

ral beauty or historic significance, whether it's a neighborhood of restored seaside mansions, a turn-of-the-20th-century artists' colony, an antique covered bridge, or a hidden farming valley. Some pass through remote hilltop settlements, while others include stunning mountain vistas or a general store with an inviting front porch to relax on. Some will beckon cyclists to lofty heights, others will appeal to those seeking an unhurried spin along a winding river or peaceful dirt road. Regardless of their appeal, the routes share a common thread: each offers the reward of exploring those off-the-beaten-path kinds of places many people never see.

Distances range from an 11-mile jaunt along the Connecticut River to a challenging 83-mile tour of New Hampshire's northernmost reaches. Each ride is designed to be completed in one day; however, the Great North Woods route and the three-state tour through the Connecticut River valley could be stretched into two or three easier days. Lodging options are included in those ride descriptions. A few of the rides drift into Maine, Vermont, and Massachusetts. Most of the rides in the Connecticut River valley section of the book include river crossings—often on historic covered bridges—that lead to scenic back roads in Vermont.

When considering a particular tour, read the route description carefully to decide whether the distance and terrain match your interests and, more importantly, physical ability. Information is provided on mileage, terrain, difficulty, recommended bicycle, area bicycle shops, and the presence of food and supply stops along the way. Detailed maps accompany thorough, mile-by-mile route descriptions. Bear in mind that all bike computers vary in their calibrations; therefore, the mileage listed in the tour description may differ from your own calculations. It's wise to pay close attention to landmarks and signposts as well as the map and ride description.

THE TERRAIN   New Hampshire's landscape of shoreline, river valleys, and mountains make for diverse riding conditions. Flat terrain in northern New England is rare; at best, the easiest routes in the river valleys have flat stretches punctuated with rolling hills. The beach roads are perfect for easy rides along the coast, while the mountains mix grinding upgrades and twisting descents with long, slow climbs.

I've tried to incorporate back roads that follow the state's major rivers—the Connecticut, Androscoggin, and Ammonoosuc, to name a few—and other smaller rivers that cut through the state. The river roads that follow gentle lowland terrain provide a respite in this state known for its rugged mountains, hills, and ridges. The most challenging terrain, and toughest climbing, is generally in the White Mountains; however, the Monadnocks and other smaller ranges include many tight, compact ridges. Even the Lakes Region is dominated by hills.

When enjoying these rides through New Hampshire's most rural areas, keep in mind a truism regarding back roads in the country: They are often narrow and winding, with little or no shoulder for cyclists to ride on. Moreover, motorists using these lightly traveled byways may not expect to encounter a cyclist around the corner, or may be unaccustomed to sharing the road. Remember to make yourself as visible as possible and ride predictably and responsibly.

BICYCLE SAFETY   If you do nothing else to protect yourself, wear a helmet. It will dramatically reduce the risk of a serious head injury—by 85 percent, according to the Bicycling Helmet Safety Institute—in the event of a fall or collision. New Hampshire has no state law requiring helmet use, so take it upon yourself to stay safe.

Always be aware of your surroundings and be prepared for the unexpected, whether it's a loose dog, a road hazard, or a car pulling into traffic or turning in front of you. Be especially careful when crossing railroad tracks or, in the case of many of these routes, riding across the wooden planks of a covered bridge.

Make yourself as visible as possible to drivers and pedestrians by wearing bright clothing. A bike light and reflectors are a good idea, especially if you tend to ride early or late in the day. Ride in single file in the same direction as traffic. When approaching a pedestrian from behind, keep in mind that a bicycle is virtually silent. You can easily startle someone who doesn't see or hear you coming, so make your presence known well in advance and leave as much room as possible when passing.

Motorists already have a lot to pay attention to, along with distractions from cell phones, children, or the radio, not to mention New Hampshire's jaw-dropping scenery and fiery autumn foliage. Therefore, it's wise to maintain the assumption that they can't see you. But drivers and cyclists should not ignore each other; use clear hand signals and establish eye contact whenever possible to make your intentions known.

HELPFUL HINTS   It's every cyclist's responsibility to plan ahead and be self-sufficient at all times. Carry plenty of food and water, as well as the tools and supplies needed to change a flat tire or do minor repairs. Bring along a spare tube, patch kit, air pump, and tire levers, and know how to use them.

Before trying any of these routes, thoroughly read the ride description so you know the area you're riding in, and note whether there are places for food and supplies along the way. Before you leave, check the map and the weather forecast. If you're riding alone, let someone know your route and how long you plan to be out. Remember that weather conditions—or your own physical condition—may make a ride longer than you anticipate.

Keeping your bike well maintained is key to how it performs on a ride. Bring it to a bike shop each spring or fall for a full tune-up. Before a ride, you (or a bike mechanic) should inspect your bike and do the following:

- Check tire pressure, tread, and sidewalls for wear; add air if tire pressure is low.
- Spray lubricant on a dry or squeaky chain.
- Check your brakes; replace pads and cables that are worn or frayed. Tighten the saddle and handlebars if they twist when pulled on.
- Spin the wheels and make adjustments if they wobble or rub against the brake pads.

FURTHER READING AND RESOURCES
Publications

Bicycling magazine
Box 7308
Red Oak, IA 51591-0308
1-800-666-2806
web site: www.bicyclingmagazine.com

Velo News magazine
1830 North 55th Street
Boulder, CO 80301-2700
web site: www.velonews.com

New Hampshire Atlas & Gazetteer
DeLorme Publishing Company
P. O. Box 298

Yarmouth, ME 04096
207-846-7000
web site: www.delorme.com
Provides topographical maps of New Hampshire in 53 detailed sections. The atlas can be found in most bookstores around New England.

New Hampshire Bicycle Clubs

Granite State Wheelmen
Box 216
Salem, NH 03079-3309
603-898-5479
web site: www.granitestatewheelmen.org

Sunapee-Banagans Bike Club
web site:www.sunapeebanagans.com
A local road- and mountain biking club that serves cyclists in western and central New Hampshire and east-central Vermont with a full schedule of group rides, training rides, and races.

Franklin-Hampshire Freewheelers Cycling Club
413-548-9435
web site: www.freewheelers.org
A Massachusetts-based club that hosts rides in New Hampshire.

New Hampshire Cycling Club
web site: www.nhcyclingclub.com
Promotes amateur competitive bicycling; hosts weekly training races.

Bicycling Organizations and Advocacy Groups

Bike Coalition of New Hampshire
Box 230
Stratham, NH 03885
web site: www.bikenewhampshire.org
Statewide bicycling advocacy organization working to create bike-friendly communities and legislation; promotes cycling for family fun, fitness, and as a means of transportation.

Seacoast Area Bicycle Routes (SABR)
Box 412
Durham, NH 03824
web site: www.seacoastbikes.com
*Promotes safe bike transportation in the seacoast region of south-
ern New Hampshire, and raises awareness of cycling as a viable
means of transportation.*

The Rails-to-Trails Conservancy
1100 17th Street (10th floor) NW
Washington, D.C. 20036
202-331-9696
web site: www.railtrails.org
*A nonprofit public policy organization devoted to converting aban-
doned railbeds into bicycle routes and multi-use trails. The country's largest trails organization, trail building, advocacy, and
public education group. The conservancy has included the
Ashuelot Rail Trail in southwestern New Hampshire among a list
of the nation's 12 top bike trails.*

League of American Bicyclists
1612 K Street NW, Suite 401
Washington, D.C. 20006-2802
202-822-1333
web site: www.bikeleague.org
*Founded in 1880 as the League of American Wheelmen. Promotes
cycling for recreation, fitness, and transportation. Devoted to advocacy, safety, and education at the local, state, and national levels.*

National Center for Bicycling & Walking
1506 21st Street NW, Suite 200
Washington, D.C. 20036
202-463-6622
web site: www.bikefed.org
*A national organization dedicated to assisting state and local
cycling-advocacy groups to obtain federal funds for bike projects
and establish cycling-related public policies. Founded as the
Bicycle Federation of America.*

SOUTHERN
NEW HAMPSHIRE:
THE SEACOAST TO
THE MONADNOCKS

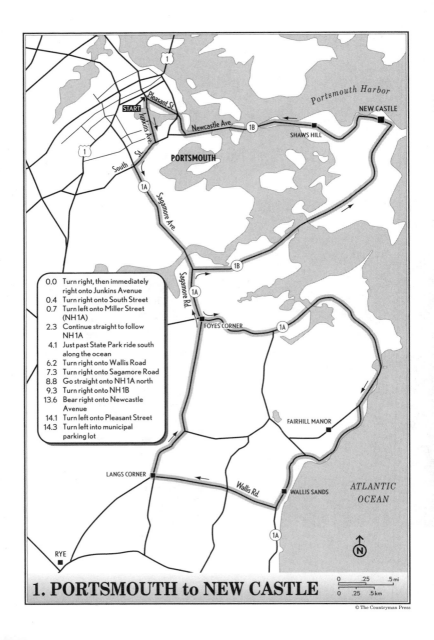

0.0	Turn right, then immediately right onto Junkins Avenue
0.4	Turn right onto South Street
0.7	Turn left onto Miller Street (NH 1A)
2.3	Continue straight to follow NH 1A
4.1	Just past State Park ride south along the ocean
6.2	Turn right onto Wallis Road
7.3	Turn right onto Sagamore Road
8.8	Go straight onto NH 1A north
9.3	Turn right onto NH 1B
13.6	Bear right onto Newcastle Avenue
14.1	Turn left onto Pleasant Street
14.3	Turn left into municipal parking lot

1. PORTSMOUTH to NEW CASTLE

0   .25   .5 mi
0   .25   .5 km

© The Countryman Press

Portsmouth to New Castle

- **DISTANCE**: 14.3 miles
- **TERRAIN**: Flat roads connected by rolling hills
- **DIFFICULTY**: Easy
- **RECOMMENDED BICYCLE**: Touring/road bike

This ride leaves the historic seaside city of Portsmouth on a tour of what's fast becoming extinct: seaside country. Portsmouth is a 17th-century fishing, farming, and shipbuilding city that in recent years has been revitalized by a downtown packed with gourmet restaurants and trendy shops. Its watery outskirts are a scenic mix of harbors, marshes, seashore, tidewater inlets, the Atlantic Ocean, and the Piscataqua River, one of the fastest navigable rivers on Earth.

Some of North America's first sawmills were erected in the communities along the Piscataqua in the early 1600s. By 1706 there were 70 water-powered mills in the Portsmouth area. Many of these processed white pine, which was harvested from the surrounding forest, then shipped across the Atlantic to the used as masts on ships in the English navy.

The tour features an endless string of water views—you'll even take a bridge across the Piscataqua to the Colonial village of New Castle, a tiny island community that seems untouched by time. In other areas the route winds inland along back roads that are far from secluded, yet remarkably quiet for such a popular and densely populated area along the Atlantic.

Much of New Hampshire's rocky shore is protected by state parks, and this ride passes one of the best—137-acre Odiorne Point State Park, the site of New Hampshire's first European settlement in 1623. Later, prominent residents built seaside mansions here, which were eventually replaced by a World War II–era fort. You can picnic and enjoy views of the ocean and Portsmouth Harbor from one of many tables lining the coast.

The 17th-century village of New Castle sits on picturesque Great Island, with its historic buildings, lobster pounds, rural coast roads, and all manner of boats, from yachts to fishing trawlers. Its settlement in 1623 as a fishing community makes New Castle one of the oldest towns in America.

A U.S. Coast Guard station is located at Fort Constitution, a former military post at the entrance to Portsmouth Harbor. It dates to the 1600s, but is most significant for its American

A view of Portsmouth Harbor from New Castle

Revolution and Civil War history. An 18th-century raid by locals is considered one of the earliest acts of aggression against England, carried out months before the actual war began.

Once back in Portsmouth, you'll likely want to do some exploring on foot. It's the oldest city in New Hampshire and, naturally, full of history. The Strawbery Banke settlement—named for the wild berries that covered the banks of the Piscataqua River centuries ago—features many well-preserved homes from as early as the 1600s. Many of the 42 buildings are on their original foundations, and the 350-year-old site is maintained as a museum with a year-round schedule of exhibits and demonstrations.

You might want to just enjoy the lively waterfront shopping and dining district, roughly in the area of Market, Ceres, and Bow Streets. You can also catch a street fair or music festival, picnic in Prescott Park, or take a cruise to the Isles of Shoals, a collection of historic islands 6 miles east of Portsmouth whose surrounding waters are full of whales and legends of pirate treasure. The islands are visible from Route 1A and Fort Constitution.

DIRECTIONS FOR THE RIDE

The ride begins in downtown Portsmouth, at the municipal parking lot off Pleasant Street, adjacent to South Mill Pond and across from the historic Governor John Langdon House.

0.0 Turn right out of the parking lot, then take an immediate right onto Junkins Avenue.
Pass South Mill Pond and the brick City Hall/police department complex.

0.4 At the stop sign, turn right onto South Street.

0.7 At the traffic light, turn left onto Miller Street (NH 1A).
The road climbs past a sprawling cemetery then rolls up and down gentle hills. When you reach the bridge over Sagamore Creek, dismount and walk your bike across.

2.3 At the four-way intersection, continue straight to follow NH 1A.
There is little or no shoulder on this narrow, twisting road, so use appropriate caution. In about a mile, you'll enter the marshland surrounding Odiorne Point, an indication that the seacoast is near.

4.1 Just past Odiorne Point State Park, start riding south along the ocean.
*This breathtaking stretch of road hugs the Atlantic coast on the way to Wallis
Sands State Beach. This point was a stop for Native Americans migrating
through the area centuries ago. John Odiorne settled here in 1660, and the
land remained in his family until World War II. Today the University of New
Hampshire operates a nature and marine museum at the point that's popular
with families.*

6.2 Turn right onto Wallis Road, following the sign to Langs Corner.

7.3 At the stop sign, turn right onto Sagamore Road.

8.8 At the next stop sign, go straight onto NH 1A north.

9.3 Turn right onto NH 1B, following the sign to New Castle.
*This scenic stretch of road passes pristine marshes and opulent waterfront estates.
The Ice House ice-cream stand is a popular stop during the summer.*

10.3 Walk your bike over the drawbridge across Little Harbor.
*The grand 19th century Wentworth-by-the-Sea resort reopened in 2003 after
years of neglect.*

11.7 Pass the entrance to Fort Constitution.
*Here at the former Castle of William & Mary, several hundred men stole military
supplies from a British garrison in 1774, one of the first such raids of the American
Revolution. If you ride into the entrance, you'll see the white Fort Point lighthouse
and possibly some Coast Guard ships. From here you have a good view of the Isles
of Shoals several miles offshore.*

11.8 Pass through New Castle.
*A collection of 17th-, 18th-, and 19th-century homes tightly packs the narrow,
winding street that bisects the heart of the village. Outside of town, you'll ride
along the narrow causeway that crosses through Portsmouth Harbor and connects
Goat Island and Shapleigh Island to the mainland.*

13.6 At the stop sign, bear right onto Newcastle Avenue.
Meticulously restored buildings line this house-crowded Portsmouth street.

14.1 Turn left onto Pleasant Street.
*The Governor John Langdon House is a grand Georgian mansion considered one
of the finest in New England. It was built in 1784 by Langdon, who led a successful*

career as a merchant and politician before becoming governor of New Hampshire. The house and gardens are open to the public for tours.

14.3 Turn left into the municipal parking lot to end the ride.

Bicycle Shops

Papa Wheelies, 653 Islington Street, Portsmouth; 603-427-2060

Bicycle Bob's Bicycle Outlets, 990 Lafayette Road, Portsmouth; 603-436-2453

Portsmouth Rent & Ride, 37 Hanover Street, Suite #2, Portsmouth; 603-433-6777

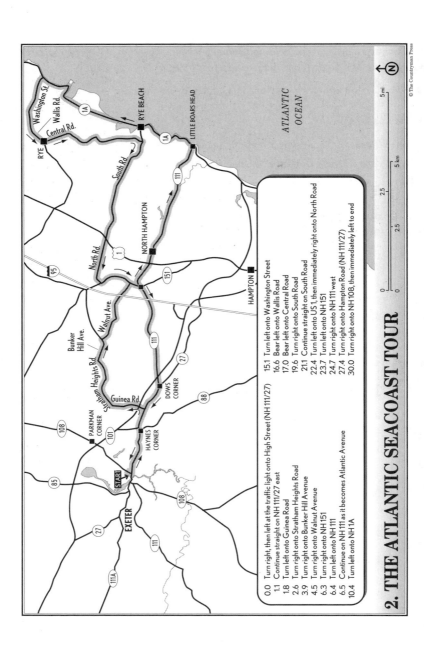

2. THE ATLANTIC SEACOAST TOUR

0.0 Turn right, then left at the traffic light onto High Street (NH 111/27)
1.1 Continue straight on NH 111/27 east
1.8 Turn left onto Guinea Road
2.6 Turn right onto Stratham Heights Road
3.9 Turn right onto Bunker Hill Avenue
4.5 Turn right onto Walnut Avenue
6.3 Turn right onto NH 151
6.4 Turn left onto NH 111
6.5 Continue on NH 111 as it becomes Atlantic Avenue
10.4 Turn left onto NH 1A
15.1 Turn left onto Washington Street
16.6 Bear left onto Wallis Road
17.0 Bear left onto Central Road
19.6 Turn right onto South Road
21.1 Continue straight on South Road
22.4 Turn left onto US 1, then immediately right onto North Road
23.7 Turn left onto NH 151
24.7 Turn right onto NH 111 west
27.4 Turn right onto Hampton Road (NH 111/27)
30.0 Turn right onto NH 108, then immediately left to end

© The Countryman Press

2

The Atlantic Seacoast Tour

- **DISTANCE:** 30 miles
- **TERRAIN:** Flat and rolling terrain; a few steep hills
- **DIFFICULTY:** Moderate
- **RECOMMENDED BICYCLE:** Touring/road bike

New Hampshire's shoreline stretches less than 20 miles along the Atlantic Ocean, but what it lacks in length it makes up for in beauty. Much of it is protected as state land, so the views are long and satisfying. Gilded mansions overlook the curved, rugged coast punctuated by rocky promontories.

To reach the ocean, you'll ride through the quiet villages of North Hampton, with its pristine white clapboard houses and regal mansions in the Little Boars Head district, and Rye, which is full of scenic back roads and surprisingly rural given its proximity to the coast.

Part of the shoreline enclave of Little Boars Head is open to the public. Fuller Gardens, the former summer home of former New Hampshire Governor Alvin Fuller, is tucked among the many glitzy estates lining the coast. People come to stroll the meticulously cared-for early-20th-century formal gardens. Many of the governor's relatives still reside in this exclusive neighborhood.

The beauty of this tour—especially the panoramic ocean views from Atlantic Avenue—draws many other visitors. For a cyclist, this means traffic. Use appropriate caution when riding, especially along the coast, when drivers' eyes may well be on the impressive scenery rather than bicycles on the road ahead.

New Hampshire's rugged coast is dotted with wide, sandy beaches.

The ride begins in Exeter, a classic New England Colonial town with an eclectic mix of cafés and shops, dressed up a bit by the presence of the prestigious Phillips Exeter Academy. For a tour that passes through downtown, see Ride 3: Exeter.

DIRECTIONS FOR THE RIDE

The ride begins at Exeter Cycles at the intersection of NH 108 and 111/27 in Exeter. You can pick up food and drinks at High Street Grocery across the street.

0.0 Turn right out of the bike shop parking lot, then left at the traffic light onto High Street (NH 111/27).
Use caution while riding through this busy residential neighborhood.

1.1 At the junction of NH 88, continue straight on NH 111/27 east.

1.8 Turn left onto Guinea Road, past Churchill's Gardens Nursery.
Cross over NH 101 and ride through a quiet neighborhood.

2.6 At the stop sign, turn right onto Stratham Heights Road.
You'll climb past hilltop farmland mixed with residential developments.

3.9 At the stop sign, turn right onto Bunker Hill Avenue.

4.5 At the next stop sign, turn right onto Walnut Avenue.
From here you'll wind back downhill toward North Hampton.

6.3 At the yield sign, turn right onto NH 151.

6.4 Turn left onto NH 111 at the white clapboard Centennial Hall on the green in North Hampton Center.

6.5 At the next stop sign, continue to follow NH 111 as it turns first left, then right to become Atlantic Avenue.

7.1 Cross US 1 and continue on NH 111, following the sign to Rye Beach.
This road is busy, but offers a wide shoulder to ride on. It's impossible to miss the barns and paddocks of Runnymede Farm, proud home to two champion race-horses, one a Kentucky Derby winner.

9.9 Pass through the Little Boars Head district just as you approach the ocean.

10.4 At the stop sign, turn left onto NH 1A and head north along the Atlantic coast.
The views to the Atlantic are impossibly dramatic, from the surf pounding the rocky shoreline to the sailboats dotting the glittering horizon. Seaside mansions appear, one seemingly more opulent than the next.

10.5 Pass the entrance for Fuller Gardens.
The Fuller Foundation maintains more than 1,500 rosebushes and perennials, as well as a Japanese garden and conservatory. The grounds are open from May through October. Beyond the gardens you'll ride past a string of beaches—including Jenness State Beach and Rye Harbor State Park—as well as sprawling tidal marshes and more modest cottages and inns.

15.1 Just past Rye Harbor State Park, turn left onto Washington Road.

16.6 At the stop sign, bear left onto Wallis Road.

17.0 In Rye, bear left at the memorial onto Central Road.
Look for the Rye Town Hall on the left.

19.6 Turn right onto South Road at the golf course.
This narrow road wends through a quiet enclave of grand homes.

21.1 At the stop sign, continue straight on South Road, following the sign for US 1.

22.4 At the next stop sign, turn left onto US 1, then make an immediate right onto North Road.

23.7 At the stop sign, turn left onto NH 151.
Use caution: This busy road has a narrow shoulder.

24.7 In North Hampton Center, turn right onto NH 111 west.

27.4 At the stop sign, turn right onto Hampton Road (NH 111/27).

30.0 At the traffic light, turn right onto NH 108, then immediately left into the parking lot of Exeter Cycles to end the ride.

Bicycle Shops

Exeter Cycles, 4 Portsmouth Avenue, Exeter; 603-778-2331

3

Exeter

- **DISTANCE:** 14.2 miles
- **TERRAIN:** Rolling hills
- **DIFFICULTY:** Easy to moderate
- **RECOMMENDED BICYCLE:** Touring/road bike

Exeter is a small coastal-area town, best known for its rich political history and as home to the prestigious prep school, Phillips Exeter Academy. The school, founded in 1783, is widely considered to be one of the nation's best, and boasts an illustrious roster of alumni, President George H. W. Bush among them. It was here, in the years before the Civil War, that the Republican party was formed.

The Front Street Historic District is chock full of cafés serving everything from gourmet vegetarian to sushi and shops selling books, crafts, and antiques. Phillips Exeter's ivy-covered campus boasts a variety of architectural styles, from Colonial and Victorian to contemporary. Exeter has a fine collection of vintage Colonial-era homes; some, like the 1868 Moses Kent House and the Gilman Garrison House, which dates to the 17th century, are open to the public.

Exeter was one of New Hampshire's earliest communities, established in 1638 along the banks of the Squamscott River. It was the state capital during the American Revolution, so naturally there is a museum celebrating American Independence here, exhibiting centuries-old artifacts, including draft copies of the Declaration of Independence and the U.S. Constitution, in a house that was a

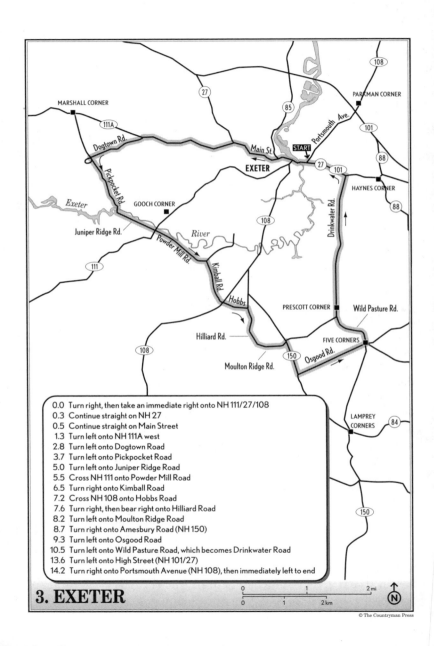

MARSHALL CORNER

PARKMAN CORNER

Dogtown Rd.

Main St.

START

EXETER

Pickpocket Rd.

Exeter

GOOCH CORNER

Juniper Ridge Rd.

River

Powder Mill Rd.

Kimball Rd.

Portsmouth Ave.

Drinkwater Rd.

HAYNES CORNER

Hobbs

PRESCOTT CORNER

Wild Pasture Rd.

FIVE CORNERS

Hilliard Rd.

Osgood Rd.

Moulton Ridge Rd.

LAMPREY CORNERS

0.0 Turn right, then take an immediate right onto NH 111/27/108
0.3 Continue straight on NH 27
0.5 Continue straight on Main Street
1.3 Turn left onto NH 111A west
2.8 Turn left onto Dogtown Road
3.7 Turn left onto Pickpocket Road
5.0 Turn left onto Juniper Ridge Road
5.5 Cross NH 111 onto Powder Mill Road
6.5 Turn right onto Kimball Road
7.2 Cross NH 108 onto Hobbs Road
7.6 Turn right, then bear right onto Hilliard Road
8.2 Turn left onto Moulton Ridge Road
8.7 Turn right onto Amesbury Road (NH 150)
9.3 Turn left onto Osgood Road
10.5 Turn left onto Wild Pasture Road, which becomes Drinkwater Road
13.6 Turn left onto High Street (NH 101/27)
14.2 Turn right onto Portsmouth Avenue (NH 108), then immediately left to end

3. EXETER

0   1   2 mi
0   1   2 km

N

© The Countryman Press

former governor's residence. The village celebrates its Revolutionary War ties over Fourth of July weekend with militia encampments and battle reenactments.

The route follows beautiful rural roads on the outskirts of Exeter and neighboring Kensington, farming communities that are fast becoming residential, thanks to a massive housing boom in the Portsmouth metropolitan area in recent years. Pedaling the back roads, one still sees sugarhouses, dairies, pastures, and barns, a nod to the area's agricultural roots.

DIRECTIONS FOR THE RIDE

The ride begins at Exeter Cycles, at the junction of NH 108 and 111. Food and drinks can be found at the High Street Grocery across the street from the bike shop.

0.0 Turn right out of the parking lot, then take an immediate right at the traffic light onto NH 111/27/108.
Once you cross the Squamscott River you'll be at the heart of this upscale New England town, whose bustling center is crammed with shops and cafés. Use caution when riding through, but notice the diverse array of architectural design in the historic buildings.

0.3 At the bandstand in the center of town, continue straight on NH 27.
The classic white bandstand was designed by internationally acclaimed sculptor Daniel Chester French. Among his best-known works are the seated statue at the Lincoln Memorial in Washington, D.C. and the Minute Man statue in Concord, Massachusetts.

0.5 Continue straight on Main Street at Phillips Exeter Academy (Water Street veers to the right).

1.3 Turn left onto NH 111A west, following the sign to Brentwood.
This quiet, tree-lined neighborhood street quickly becomes a rural country road that winds through the woods.

2.8 Turn left onto Dogtown Road.

3.7 At the stop sign, turn left onto Pickpocket Road.
You'll ride past vintage homes and bucolic farms, even a small airport, on this back road.

The historic buildings in downtown Exeter reflect a rich architectural diversity.

5.0 Turn left onto Juniper Ridge Road.

5.5 At the stop sign, cross NH 111 onto Powder Mill Road.
This isolated stretch is mostly farmland, with some woodland and a few open meadows.

6.5 Turn right onto Kimball Road.

7.2 At the stop sign, cross NH 108 onto Hobbs Road.
Notice the nicely restored homes as you climb past open fields on the outskirts of Shaws Hill Farm.

7.6 At the T-intersection, turn right, make a short descent, then bear right onto Hilliard Road.

8.2 At the stop sign, turn left onto Moulton Ridge Road.

8.7 At the next stop sign, turn right onto Amesbury Road (NH 150).

You'll pass a café and convenience store on this road. NH 150 was one of the area's earliest roads, laid out in 1739.

9.3 At the white clapboard Kensington Town Hall, turn left onto Osgood Road.

10.5 At the stop sign, turn left onto Wild Pasture Road.
This flat stretch of rural road cuts through a landscape of horse pastures, farms, stone walls, and barns. It turns into Drinkwater Road as you cross back into Exeter.

13.6 At the yield sign, turn left onto High Street (NH 101/27).

14.2 At the traffic light, turn right onto Portsmouth Avenue (NH 108), then immediately left into the parking lot of Exeter Cycles to end the ride.

Bicycle Shops

Exeter Cycles, 4 Portsmouth Avenue, Exeter; 603-778-2331

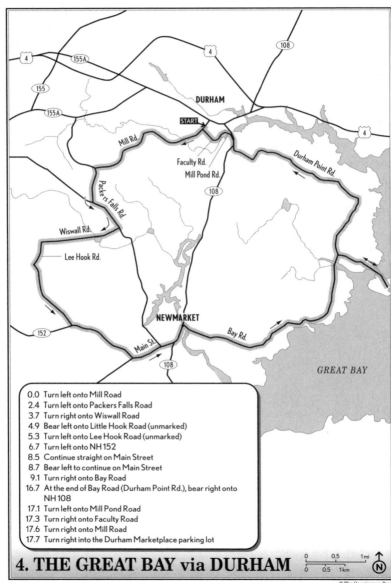

0.0 Turn left onto Mill Road
2.4 Turn left onto Packers Falls Road
3.7 Turn right onto Wiswall Road
4.9 Bear left onto Little Hook Road (unmarked)
5.3 Turn left onto Lee Hook Road (unmarked)
6.7 Turn left onto NH 152
8.5 Continue straight on Main Street
8.7 Bear left to continue on Main Street
9.1 Turn right onto Bay Road
16.7 At the end of Bay Road (Durham Point Rd.), bear right onto
     NH 108
17.1 Turn left onto Mill Pond Road
17.3 Turn right onto Faculty Road
17.6 Turn right onto Mill Road
17.7 Turn right into the Durham Marketplace parking lot

4. THE GREAT BAY via DURHAM

0   0.5   1 mi
0   0.5 1 km

N

The Great Bay via Durham and Newmarket

- **DISTANCE:** 17.7 miles
- **TERRAIN:** Rolling hills
- **DIFFICULTY:** Moderate
- **RECOMMENDED BICYCLE:** Touring/road bike

Durham is a college town that revolves around the institution to which it plays host. The University of New Hampshire and its twelve thousand students support a good selection of restaurants and shops and, during the academic year, a full schedule of art exhibits and theatrical, dance, and musical performances at the Paul Creative Arts Center.

You'll ride around Great Bay, a large-yet-shallow tidal bay spread across 4,500 acres of tidal wetlands, inlets, and marshland. This fragile environment is unique in an area of farmland that's rapidly being carved into residential communities. It's all part of the Great Bay National Estuarine Research Reserve, a protected area rich in wildlife, birds—including nesting bald eagles—oysters, fish, and two dozen endangered species. This is an excellent area in which to view shorebirds. The Piscataqua River drains and fills the bay according to the tides at Portsmouth Harbor. An optional side trip takes you to Adams Point, home to the UNH Jackson Estuarine Lab. The scenic point is a good picnic spot, and there's even a self-guided nature trail with stunning views.

Newmarket is a historic brick-and-granite mill town on Great Bay and the Lamprey and Piscassic Rivers. In the 19th century, this was a busy industrial center. Today it offers a handful of places to eat and shop. In between villages you'll find rolling countryside dotted with farmland, thick woods, and fields.

DIRECTIONS FOR THE RIDE
The ride begins in downtown Durham at the Durham Marketplace plaza on Mill Road.

0.0 Turn left from the parking lot onto Mill Road.
Pass by some UNH campus buildings, then through a tree-lined neighborhood.

2.4 At the stop sign, turn left onto Packers Falls Road.
This rolling road cuts across open farmland that features antique homesteads and new developments.

3.7 At the stop sign, turn right onto Wiswall Road.

4.0 Cross a one-lane bridge over the Little River.
From here, you'll gradually climb past fields, barns, and old-time farms.

4.9 At the stop sign, bear left onto Little Hook Road (unmarked).

5.3 At the stop sign, turn left onto Lee Hook Road (unmarked).

6.7 At the next stop sign, turn left onto NH 152, heading east toward Newmarket.

8.5 At the brick Newmarket Town Hall, continue straight on Main Street.

8.7 At the stop sign and blinking traffic light, bear left to continue on Main Street.
This well-preserved brick mill town has an assortment of cafés serving coffee, ice cream, and meals, as well as shops and a bookstore.

9.1 Cross the Lamprey River, then turn right onto Bay Road.
Pass behind a cluster of mills, many of which have been converted into condominiums and office space, and the modest dwellings built decades ago as worker housing. The road narrows and winds past memorable views of Great Bay and its sprawling marshes and tidal inlets. The rambling stone walls mixed with woods hint at the area's agricultural past.

Great Bay has many quiet rural roads perfect for cycling.

13.0 Optional side trip: Just past the small bridge through a marsh is Adams Point Road, which leads to the Jackson Estuarine Laboratory.
Located at the tip of mile-long Adams Point Wildlife Management Area, this UNH lab has been conducting experiments for more than 30 years. A self-guided nature trail and a picnic area at this pristine point on Great Bay make for a relaxing stop.

16.7 At the end of Bay Road (called Durham Point Road when you reenter Durham), bear right at the yield sign onto NH 108.

17.1 Turn left onto Mill Pond Road.

17.3 At the stop sign, turn right onto Faculty Road.

17.6 At the stop sign, turn right onto Mill Road.

17.7 Turn right into the Durham Marketplace parking lot to end the ride.

Bicycle Shops

Durham Bike, Pettee Brook Lane, Durham; 603-868-5634

5

Hill Villages: Bennington, Francestown, Greenfield

- **DISTANCE:** 27 miles
- **TERRAIN:** Rolling and steep hills; about 5 miles of dirt road
- **DIFFICULTY:** Strenuous
- **RECOMMENDED BICYCLE:** Mountain bike/hybrid

This tour passes through a trio of historic villages on thickly forested roads. If you're looking for isolation and solitude, you'll enjoy this ride through the rural, lofty Monadnocks. What these communities have in common, besides the old-time homesteads, Colonial buildings, and general stores of quintessential New England, is a landscape laced with stone walls and patchwork fields. The hulk of Crotched Mountain provides a dramatic backdrop and serves as a reminder that you're riding deep into hill country.

Francestown, named for the wife of 18th-century governor John Wentworth, is a charming, well-preserved village without touristy frills. Once a commercial center, today it's a sleepy residential hamlet. In its heyday, the town bustled with a variety of mills, as well as craftsmen, blacksmiths, and other industries, particularly the quarrying of soapstone. The town hall building is the former Francestown Academy, once a premier academic institution with an illustrious list of alumni that includes a U.S. president (Franklin Pierce) and high-ranking government leaders. The 1814 general store is the hub of the village, which also has a good number of graceful Federal-era homes lining the street into town.

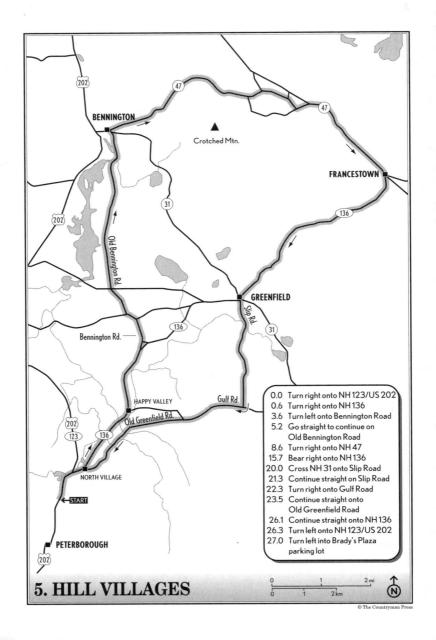

0.0	Turn right onto NH 123/US 202
0.6	Turn right onto NH 136
3.6	Turn left onto Bennington Road
5.2	Go straight to continue on Old Bennington Road
8.6	Turn right onto NH 47
15.7	Bear right onto NH 136
20.0	Cross NH 31 onto Slip Road
21.3	Continue straight on Slip Road
22.3	Turn right onto Gulf Road
23.5	Continue straight onto Old Greenfield Road
26.1	Continue straight onto NH 136
26.3	Turn left onto NH 123/US 202
27.0	Turn left into Brady's Plaza parking lot

BENNINGTON

Crotched Mtn.

FRANCESTOWN

Old Bennington Rd.

GREENFIELD

Slip Rd.

Bennington Rd.

Gulf Rd.

HAPPY VALLEY

Old Greenfield Rd.

NORTH VILLAGE

START

PETERBOROUGH

5. HILL VILLAGES

0   1   2 mi
0   1   2 km

N

Bennington has several well-preserved vintage buildings, including the Congregational church and town hall. Like Francestown, this village was an industrial hub long ago, with tanneries and several mills, including New England's first cotton mill.

Greenfield is another 18th-century gem, boasting the state's oldest original meetinghouse to serve as both church and town hall. Like historic buildings across New England it was built of modest clapboard, but dressed up with stained glass windows. After two hundred years, it's still used by Greenfield's townsfolk.

The lively community of Peterborough, incorporated in 1760, is about a mile from this tour, and a worthwhile post-ride stop. It's long been a haven for artists, writers, and other creative types. Stroll Grove and Main Streets, take in a performance by the Peterborough Players, a summer theater group that has staged shows here for more than 50 years, or listen to the Monadnock Music chamber orchestra. The public library here is the nation's first tax-funded free library.

DIRECTIONS FOR THE RIDE

The ride begins in the parking lot of Brady's Plaza, about a mile north of downtown Peterborough on NH 123/US 202.

0.0 Turn right out of the parking lot onto NH 123/US 202.

0.6 Turn right onto NH 136, heading east toward Greenfield.
This road cuts a swath through rolling hills mixed with woods and farmland.

3.6 Turn left onto Bennington Road.

5.2 At the stop sign, go straight to continue on Old Bennington Road.
The road surface is dirt for the next 2 miles. You'll pass few homes as you climb and descend the rolling hills on the outskirts of Greenfield.

7.2 Cross a set of railroad tracks at the Bennington town line.
The road returns to pavement here.

8.5 At the stop sign, continue straight into the village of Bennington.
The Bennington Country Store is a good place to pick up supplies or take a break; it has a market and deli.

The hills around Greenfield, Bennington, and Francestown are laced with back roads.

8.6 Turn right onto NH 47 toward Francestown.
This quiet road rolls up and down thickly wooded hills.

15.5 Pass through the tiny village of Francestown.
The rambling clapboard Francestown Village Store has a deli and sells grocery items. Notice the graceful architecture of the historic homes lining the street into town.

15.7 Bear right onto NH 136, heading west toward Greenfield.
The rural, wooded countryside between the villages is rugged and hilly.

20.0 At the blinking traffic light in Greenfield, cross NH 31 onto Slip Road.
The roads are unpaved until you reach the Peterborough town line, about 3 miles from here.

21.3 At the junction of Slip Road and Zephyr Lake Road, continue straight on Slip Road.

22.3 At the T-intersection, turn right onto Gulf Road.

23.2 At the unmarked Peterborough town line, the road is once again paved.

23.5 At the junction of Holt Street, continue straight onto Old Greenfield Road.

26.1 At the stop sign, continue straight onto NH 136.

26.3 At the next stop sign, turn left onto NH 123/US 202.

27.0 Turn left into the parking lot of Brady's Plaza to end the ride.

Bicycle Shops

Eclectic Bicycle, 109 Grove Street, Peterborough; 603-924-9797

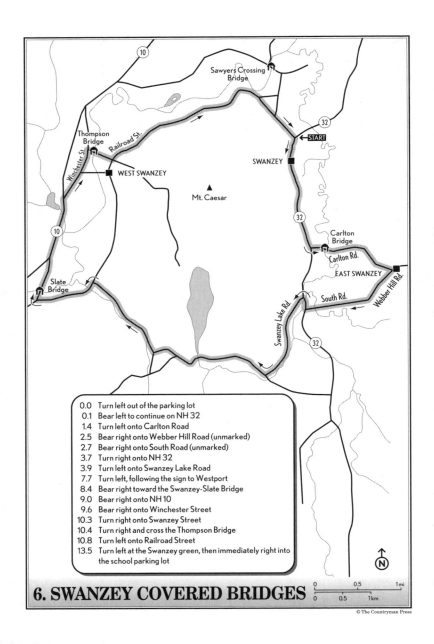

0.0	Turn left out of the parking lot
0.1	Bear left to continue on NH 32
1.4	Turn left onto Carlton Road
2.5	Bear right onto Webber Hill Road (unmarked)
2.7	Bear right onto South Road (unmarked)
3.7	Turn right onto NH 32
3.9	Turn left onto Swanzey Lake Road
7.7	Turn left, following the sign to Westport
8.4	Bear right toward the Swanzey-Slate Bridge
9.0	Bear right onto NH 10
9.6	Bear right onto Winchester Street
10.3	Turn right onto Swanzey Street
10.4	Turn right and cross the Thompson Bridge
10.8	Turn left onto Railroad Street
13.5	Turn left at the Swanzey green, then immediately right into the school parking lot

6. SWANZEY COVERED BRIDGES

0   0.5   1mi
0   0.5   1km

© The Countryman Press

Swanzey Covered Bridges

- **DISTANCE:** 13.5 miles
- **TERRAIN:** Flat roads and rolling hills
- **DIFFICULTY:** Easy
- **RECOMMENDED BICYCLE:** Touring/road bike

One of New Hampshire's best and most surprising secrets is its superb collection of vintage covered bridges. These historic structures—an astounding 64 of them—evoke a bygone era, Currier and Ives images of carriages and sleighs being whisked through old New England villages by high-stepping horses.

At one time there were close to four hundred covered bridges in New Hampshire. Many of the remaining wooden bridges, also known as "courting bridges" and "kissing bridges," have been refurbished and still carry automobile traffic across rivers and streams. Others are open to pedestrians only, sometimes moved to the side of the road or to a state park. Each is unique, whether in color, size, history, or architectural style. These bridges were covered not so much for the aesthetic appeal, but to protect the wooden trusses from the elements. One is the longest covered bridge in the United States (see Ride 12: Windsor, Vermont, via the Cornish-Windsor covered Bridge), while another is the country's oldest railroad covered bridge (see Ride 10: Bradford, Henniker, Warner: A Monadnock/Merrimack Tour).

The rural countryside south of Keene is home to more covered bridges than anyplace else in the state, and this tour takes you over four of these vintage structures. The first is the Swanzey-Carlton Bridge, which spans the South Branch of the Ashuelot River. Next is the Swanzey-Slate Bridge, an 1860s red clapboard bridge featuring a sign announcing a five-dollar fine "for riding or driving over this bridge faster than a walk."

The red clapboard Thompson Bridge was built in 1832 over the Ashuelot River in West Swanzey. A side trip leads to the 1859 Cresson Bridge, also known as the Swanzey–Sawyers Crossing Bridge, in Swanzey village. In West Swanzey, the Swanzey Historical Museum offers maps to the area's bridges. There are several other covered bridges in the vicinity, including a pair in Winchester and another near Greenfield.

DIRECTIONS FOR THE RIDE

The ride begins at Monadnock Regional Junior-Senior High School on Old Homestead Highway (NH 32) in East Swanzey. When school is in session, find a parking place in Swanzey.

0.0 Turn left out of the parking lot and head toward the intersection.

0.1 Bear left to continue on NH 32.
Pass through the tiny Colonial village of Swanzey, whose cluster of vintage buildings includes a town hall, grange, library, and church. This scenic country road is relatively flat and makes for easy, enjoyable riding.

1.4 Turn left onto Carlton Road at the sign for Covered Bridge #7.
The red clapboard Carlton Bridge was built over the South Branch of the Ashuelot River in 1789 and reconstructed in 1869. Notice the beautiful mountain ranges in the distance.

2.5 At the unmarked intersection, bear right onto Webber Hill Road.

2.7 At the stop sign, bear right onto South Road (unmarked) at the Swanzey Fire Station.

3.7 At the stop sign, turn right onto NH 32.

3.9 Turn left onto Swanzey Lake Road.
Thickly wooded rolling hills afford occasional glimpses of open meadows.

7.7 Turn left at the stop sign, following the sign to Westport.

The Thompson Covered Bridge in West Swanzey was built across the Ashuelot River in the 1830s.

8.4 At the yield sign, bear right toward the Swanzey-Slate Bridge.

9.0 At the stop sign, bear right onto NH 10.
A gas station/convenience store here sells food and drinks. Use caution on this heavily traveled road.

9.6 Bear right onto Winchester Street.
This neighborhood marks the outskirts of the tiny mill village of West Swanzey.

10.3 Turn right onto Swanzey Street, just past the brick mill complex.

10.4 At the yield sign, turn right and cross the Ashuelot River on the Thompson Bridge.
This 155-foot covered bridge, also known as the Swanzey–West Swanzey Bridge, has a pedestrian walkway. After crossing the river, ride up a short hill that cuts through the center of town.

10.8 Turn left at the intersection onto Railroad Street.

13.0 Optional side trip: To see the Cresson Covered Bridge, also called the

Swanzey–Sawyers Crossing Bridge, turn left onto Sawyers Crossing Road and ride for about a half mile. The 1859 bridge spans the Ashuelot River upstream of the Thompson Bridge. Retrace your way to rejoin the route.

13.5 Turn left at the Swanzey green, then immediately right into the school parking lot to end the ride.

Bicycle Shops

Banagan's Cycling Company, 82 Main Street, Keene; 603-357-2331; www.banagans.com

7

Western Monadnock Villages

- **DISTANCE:** 31.6 miles
- **TERRAIN:** Rolling and steep hills
- **DIFFICULTY:** Strenuous
- **RECOMMENDED BICYCLE:** Touring/road bike

This tour cuts through the remote hills east of the Connecticut River. You'll visit a string of sleepy New England villages that are part of the popular Monadnock Region, yet off the beaten tourist track. Despite the passage of time, these places still look just as they have for the past two centuries.

Marlow, Alstead, Drewsville, Langdon, and Acworth seem caught in a delightful time warp. The heart of Marlow is a small grassy triangle surrounded by assorted 18th- and 19th-century buildings on Village Pond. You'll pass a couple of covered bridges and a handful of working sugarhouses on your way through the hills.

Alstead is a group of three separate villages scattered amid hills and farmland. One of them, Mill Hollow, has an 18th-century mill on Lake Warren. The center of Alstead has a rambling general store and café and an elegant domed stone library. East Alstead is a lofty cluster of old homes and a handsome Congregational church.

Drewsville is actually part of Walpole's rural outskirts, a collection of hilltop buildings that includes a bustling general store. Its centerpiece is a classic common surrounded by a handsome collection of New England architecture. A narrow road allows you to ride the

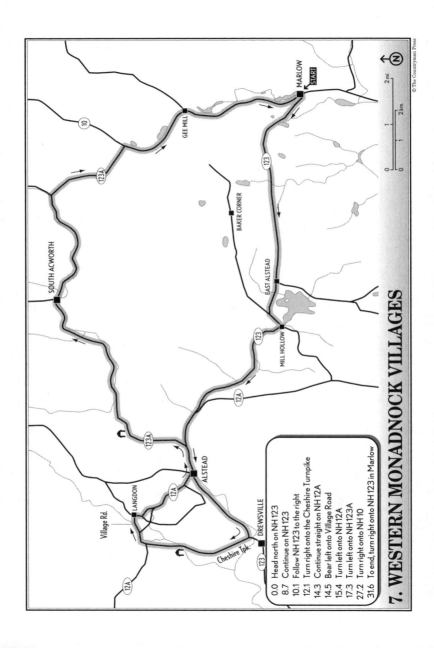

7. WESTERN MONADNOCK VILLAGES

MARLOW
START

GEE MILL

SOUTH ACWORTH

BAKER CORNER

EAST ALSTEAD

MILL HOLLOW

ALSTEAD

LANGDON

Village Rd.

DREWSVILLE

Cheshire Tpk.

10
123A
123
12A
12A

0.0   Head north on NH123
8.7   Continue on NH123
10.1   Follow NH123 to the right
12.1   Turn right onto the Cheshire Turnpike
14.3   Continue straight on NH12A
14.5   Bear left onto Village Road
15.4   Turn left onto NH12A
17.3   Turn left onto NH123A
27.2   Turn right onto NH10
31.6   To end, turn right onto NH123 in Marlow

N

0   1   2 mi
0   1   2 km

© The Countryman Press

entire perimeter and view these restored buildings up close. Farther along, up a steep hill, is the white clapboard center of Langdon, a gem you're almost guaranteed to have to yourself.

DIRECTIONS FOR THE RIDE

The ride begins at the Marlow Grocery in the village of Marlow, at the junction of NH 10 and 123. Park at the small town common across from Jones Hall, or next to the Oddfellows Hall.

0.0 From the grocery store, head north on NH 123.
The cluster of handsome old homes lining the way to East Alstead gives way to wooded rolling hills above Lake Warren. Open views of fields and distant mountains provide a scenic backdrop to 18th-century Mill Hollow and its restored water-powered mill on Camp Brook.

8.7 At the junction of NH 12A, continue on NH 123.

9.5 Pass through Alstead, staying on NH 123.
This sleepy village has a grocery store, café/hot-dog stand, and pottery studio. To the left, Main Street has seen better days, but its faded homes and grange hall are worth a quick look, if only to imagine their potential.

10.1 Follow NH 123 to the right as it passes in front of the domed, Neoclassical Revival–era Shedd-Porter Memorial Library.
Here the road follows the twists and turns of the Cold River.

12.1 At the blinking traffic light, turn right onto the Cheshire Turnpike.
Optional side trip: Turn left here and climb a half mile to the off-the-beaten-path village of Drewsville. The red clapboard general store, stone church, and collection of neat, historic homes line the long, grassy common.

13.5 Pass by the Prentiss Covered Bridge.
Rural, wide cornfields, scattered homes.

14.3 Continue straight on NH 12A, following the sign to Langdon.

14.5 Bear left off NH 12A onto Village Road.
It's a steep but short climb into Langdon.

15.0 In Langdon, follow the road to the right as it winds downhill.
This village is a mere hilltop cluster of churches and a cemetery.

15.4 At the stop sign, turn left onto NH 12A.

16.6 Follow NH 12A as it joins NH 123 in Alstead.

17.3 At the service station, turn left onto NH 123A, following the sign to Acworth.
This twisting country road hugs the Cold River, passing McDermott Covered Bridge along the way.

22.5 Pass through South Acworth, continuing on NH 123A.
The 1865 Village Store is the centerpiece of this tiny roadside hamlet. A post office, white church, and handful of historic homes complete the picture.

27.2 At the stop sign, turn right onto NH 10, heading south to Marlow.

31.6 Turn right onto NH 123 in Marlow to end the ride.

Bicycle Shops

Banagan's Cycling Company, 82 Main Street, Keene; 603-357-2331; www.banagans.com

Claremont Cyclesport, 51 Pleasant Street, Claremont; 603-542-2453; www.cyclesport.com

Outspokin' Bicycle and Sport Shop, NH 103 and 103A, Newbury, 603-763-9500; www.outspokin.com

8

Peterborough

- **DISTANCE:** 28.6 miles
- **TERRAIN:** Rolling hills and steep climbs and descents; a half-mile of dirt road
- **DIFFICULTY:** Strenuous
- **RECOMMENDED BICYCLE:** Touring/road bike

This ride features three New England villages and the woods and pastoral countryside between them. The towering 3,165-foot peak of Mount Monadnock presides over this area of rugged terrain.

Peterborough is a small but lively town with unique shops, art galleries, and restaurants lining Main Street. The presence of the many writers and artists in the area clearly influences and supports the eclectic mix. Noted New England–based writers of the 1800s such as Ralph Waldo Emerson and Henry David Thoreau wrote lovingly of the natural beauty of the area, much like they did about other New England icons that inspired them, like Mount Greylock and Walden Pond. Artists also retreated here to work; the MacDowell Colony in Peterborough became a formal colony where musicians, artists, and writers could work in uninterrupted peace, surrounded by natural beauty.

Jaffrey Center is another vintage village, with its 1773 white meetinghouse, Greek Revival schoolhouse, and charming Inn at Jaffrey Center. At nearly 1,500 feet above sea level, Dublin claims the state's loftiest town center, which is easy to believe on this high

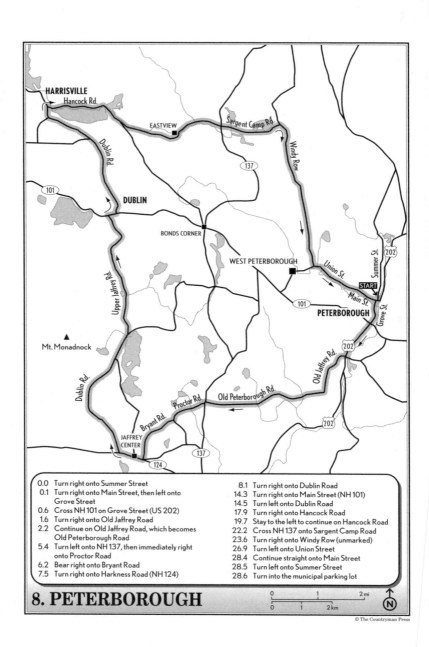

0.0   Turn right onto Summer Street
0.1   Turn right onto Main Street, then left onto
      Grove Street
0.6   Cross NH 101 on Grove Street (US 202)
1.6   Turn right onto Old Jaffrey Road
2.2   Continue on Old Jaffrey Road, which becomes
      Old Peterborough Road
5.4   Turn left onto NH 137, then immediately right
      onto Proctor Road
6.2   Bear right onto Bryant Road
7.5   Turn right onto Harkness Road (NH 124)

8.1   Turn right onto Dublin Road
14.3 Turn right onto Main Street (NH 101)
14.5 Turn left onto Dublin Road
17.9 Turn right onto Hancock Road
19.7 Stay to the left to continue on Hancock Road
22.2 Cross NH 137 onto Sargent Camp Road
23.6 Turn right onto Windy Row (unmarked)
26.9 Turn left onto Union Street
28.4 Continue straight onto Main Street
28.5 Turn left onto Summer Street
28.6 Turn into the municipal parking lot

8. PETERBOROUGH

```
0              1           2 mi
0       1        2 km
```

N

and hilly part of the tour. Like Peterborough, Dublin became a popular retreat for artists and writers at the turn of the 20th century. The village boasts a collection of 60 historic buildings, predominantly 19th-century Greek Revival and Georgian, and is perhaps best known as home base for *Yankee* magazine and *The Old Farmer's Almanac.*

Mount Monadnock was blazed with trails in the 1800s and has attracted scores of hikers ever since. They're drawn by the appealing combination of spectacular mountain views and the relatively moderate hike to the summit. It's the second-most-climbed peak in the world, trailing only Japan's Mount Fuji. You'll pedal through the state park's thickly wooded hills.

Luckily for cyclists, the quiet country roads around the park belie this popularity. The surrounding rugged Monadnock Range, covered in woodland and laced with stone walls, offers some of the most scenic riding in the state, as well as many charming inns. It's a challenging route; however, most of the climbing is tackled in the first half of the ride, leaving the rewarding descents for the end when you need them most.

DIRECTIONS FOR THE RIDE
The ride begins in the center of Peterborough at the municipal parking lot on Summer Street, next to the fire station.

0.0 Turn right out of the parking lot onto Summer Street.

0.1 At the stop sign, turn right onto Main Street, then take the first left onto Grove Street.
Use caution on this busy downtown street lined with cafés and shops.

0.6 At the traffic light, cross NH 101 onto Grove Street (US 202), following the signs for Jaffrey.
Stop in at Eclectic Bicycle for other cycling ideas in the area, or to join up with a group ride.

1.6 Turn right onto Old Jaffrey Road.
Centuries-old trees and rambling stone walls follow this scenic back road as it rolls up and down forested hills past old farms and homesteads.

New Hampshire's hills are crisscrossed with old time country lanes.

2.2 At the junction of Old Town Farm Road, stay to the left to continue on Old Jaffrey Road.
The road name changes to Old Peterborough Road at the Jaffrey town line.

5.4 At the stop sign, turn left onto NH 137, then take an immediate right onto Proctor Road.

6.2 At the Y-intersection at the crest of the hill, bear right onto Bryant Road.

7.5 At the stop sign in Jaffrey Center, turn right onto Harkness Road (NH 124).
The centerpieces of this photogenic hilltop village are the charming Inn at Jaffrey Center and the gleaming white 1773 meetinghouse, complete with soaring steeple.

8.1 Turn right onto Dublin Road, following the sign for Monadnock State Park. This turns into Upper Jaffrey Road as you cross into Dublin.

Climb past Shattuck Golf Course and through the woods, beyond Thorndike Pond and the state park entrance. There are 6 miles of climbing ahead before the descent into Dublin.

14.3 At the stop sign, turn right onto Main Street (NH 101).

14.5 Turn left onto Dublin Road, just before the town common.
A worthwhile detour just ahead on Main Street is a stop in New Hampshire's highest village center, home to Yankee Magazine and a number of centuries-old buildings. Then begin the long descent into Harrisville on Dublin Road.

17.9 Turn right onto Hancock Road.
The road hugs the remote and scenic northern shore of Skatutakee Lake.

19.7 At the junction of Bonds Corner Road, stay to the left to continue on Hancock Road.

22.2 At the stop sign, cross NH 137 onto Sargent Camp Road.
This rural forest road is unpaved for about a half mile. Down the road is Boston University's Sargent Center, an 850-acre spread laced with 12 miles of cross-country ski trails.

23.6 At the T-intersection, turn right onto Windy Row (unmarked).
Enjoy this long, wooded descent into Peterborough.

26.9 At the stop sign, turn left onto Union Street.

28.4 At the stop sign in Peterborough, continue straight onto Main Street.

28.5 Turn left onto Summer Street.

28.6 Turn into the municipal parking lot to end the ride.

Bicycle Shops

Eclectic Bicycle, 109 Grove Street, Peterborough; 603-924-9797

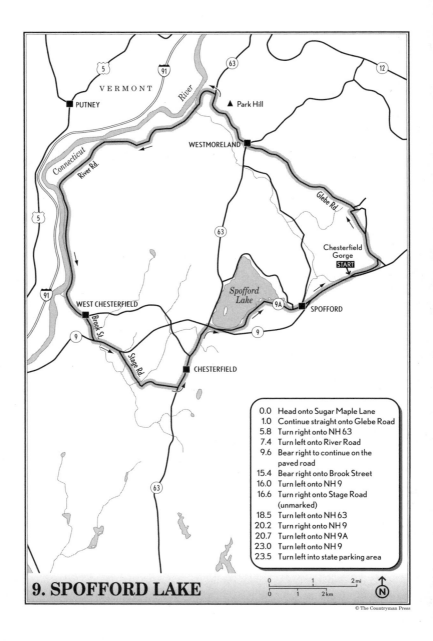

0.0	Head onto Sugar Maple Lane
1.0	Continue straight onto Glebe Road
5.8	Turn right onto NH 63
7.4	Turn left onto River Road
9.6	Bear right to continue on the paved road
15.4	Bear right onto Brook Street
16.0	Turn left onto NH 9
16.6	Turn right onto Stage Road (unmarked)
18.5	Turn left onto NH 63
20.2	Turn right onto NH 9
20.7	Turn left onto NH 9A
23.0	Turn left onto NH 9
23.5	Turn left into state parking area

9. SPOFFORD LAKE

0   1   2 mi

0   1   2 km

N

Spofford Lake via Westmoreland and Chesterfield

- **DISTANCE:** 23.5 miles
- **TERRAIN:** Rolling with a couple of steep climbs; flat stretches along the Connecticut River
- **DIFFICULTY:** Moderate to Strenuous
- **RECOMMENDED BICYCLE:** Touring/road bike

Spofford Lake is the hub of a rural residential area in southwestern New Hampshire, just shy of the Vermont border. The quiet community of Spofford is little more than a string of cottages on the lake's southern shore. Views of the shimmering water flash through the trees as you ride in this wooded area.

The tour begins at Chesterfield Gorge, a rugged natural area off busy NH 9. A half-mile trail leads through thick pines to a footbridge over the narrow, rocky chasm. You can picnic near the rushing stream that has sliced its way through a tumble of granite.

Two picture-perfect New England villages appear along the tour. Westmoreland, a quiet collection of neat clapboard buildings with a friendly country store, is tucked among undulating hills. High on a ridge, Chesterfield's grassy common and the historic buildings surrounding it look out over a patchwork of farm fields and thick woodland that stretches to the Connecticut River. This is the birthplace of Chief Justice Harlan Fiske, who was born on a country road on the rural outskirts. A historical marker by the road tells his story. The hills surrounding Chesterfield are part of Pisgah

State Park, a 13,500-acre forest laced with fishing ponds and trails for hiking and cross-country skiing.

DIRECTIONS FOR THE RIDE

The ride begins at the Chesterfield Gorge State Wayside Parking Area on NH 9, a short distance east of Spofford Lake. There are bathrooms and phones at the trailhead to the gorge; for supplies, head 6 miles east to Keene.

0.0 At the east end of the parking lot, head onto Sugar Maple Lane. *This narrow road parallels busy NH 9.*

1.0 Continue straight onto Glebe Road (behind the restaurant on NH 9). *As the road splits north from the highway, it traverses marshland before descending through the forest with views of the half-dozen or so craggy hills surrounding Westmoreland.*

A rural road on the outskirts of Westmoreland

5.8 At the stop sign in Westmoreland, turn right onto NH 63.
A cluster of historic buildings—a brick church, yellow clapboard general store, and town hall—line a picturesque town common.

7.1 Climb past the Warwick Preserve and the gleaming white 1762 Park Hill Meeting House before descending Park Hill.

7.4 Turn left onto River Road.
Past the prison, this quiet back road cuts through a long farming valley spread with cornfields and rolling meadows that stretch to the Connecticut River, with views west to the mountains of Vermont.

9.6 At the Y-intersection next to an old red schoolhouse, bear right to continue on the unmarked paved road (Pocham Road is the dirt road that goes to the left).

15.2 Pass through West Chesterfield.
This sleepy village consists of a closed general store, a tiny firehouse, and a white clapboard meetinghouse.

15.4 At the Y-intersection, bear right onto Brook Street.

16.0 At the stop sign, turn left onto NH 9.
You'll climb for about a half mile on this busy road; use caution when crossing.

16.6 Turn right onto Stage Road (unmarked).
Descend through farmland and meadows for about a mile, then climb an equal distance.

18.5 At the stop sign, turn left onto NH 63, heading north to Chesterfield.

19.0 Pass through Chesterfield.
This village sits high and proud on an open ridge surrounded by working farms, with views of the Pisgah Mountain Range.

20.2 At the stop sign, turn right onto NH 9.

20.7 Turn left onto NH 9A.
This side road takes you along the southern shore of Spofford Lake and through the tiny community of Spofford.

23.0 Turn left onto NH 9.

23.5 Turn left into the state parking area to end the ride.

Bicycle Shops

Banagan's Cycling Company, 82 Main Street, Keene; 603-357-2331; www.banagans.com

10

Bradford, Henniker, Warner: A Monadnock/Merrimack Tour

- ■ **DISTANCE:** 34.4 miles
- ■ **TERRAIN:** Rolling hills; some steep climbs and descents
- ■ **DIFFICULTY:** Strenuous
- ■ **RECOMMENDED BICYCLE:** Touring/road bike

Surrounded by Mount Sunapee, Mount Kearsage, and many rolling hills, this wooded area of rural back roads is tucked into the Contoocook River Valley. Along the way are three covered bridges and some classic New England villages.

Henniker is small and friendly, a thriving mill community turned college town. New England College was established here in the 1940s, and today the pretty campus on the banks of the Contoocook River is home to around a thousand students and faculty. It's located on the western edge of the Merrimack Valley, in a picturesque yet little-visited part of the otherwise heavily developed valley, which includes the cities of Manchester and Concord, the state capital. Henniker offers an interesting mix of restaurants, inns, and shops, a covered bridge—even a winery. It also boasts a bit of trivia: It proudly shares its name with no other town in the world.

In the 19th century, Bradford bustled with train travelers who stopped for the night on the way north to Lake Sunapee. Today, the restored railroad depot on NH 114 is home to a restaurant and bakery, still a popular stop with vacationers en route to the lake.

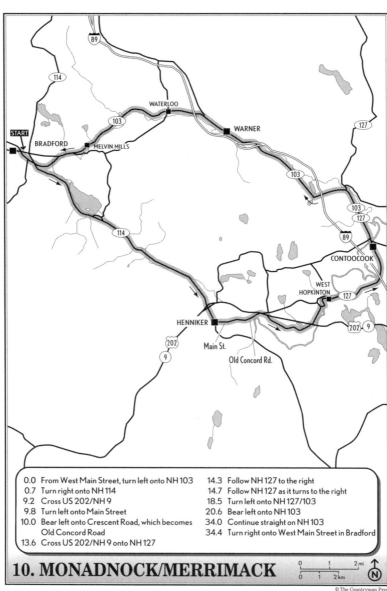

0.0 From West Main Street, turn left onto NH 103
0.7 Turn right onto NH 114
9.2 Cross US 202/NH 9
9.8 Turn left onto Main Street
10.0 Bear left onto Crescent Road, which becomes Old Concord Road
13.6 Cross US 202/NH 9 onto NH 127

14.3 Follow NH 127 to the right
14.7 Follow NH 127 as it turns to the right
18.5 Turn left onto NH 127/103
20.6 Bear left onto NH 103
34.0 Continue straight on NH 103
34.4 Turn right onto West Main Street in Bradford

10. MONADNOCK/MERRIMACK

0   1   2 mi
0   1   2 km

N

© The Countryman Press

The rural village of Warner is home to the Mount Kearsage Indian Museum, which maintains an extensive collection of Native American artifacts from around the country. Every autumn thousands of leaf peepers converge on this tiny community for its popular Fall Foliage Festival. Covered bridge enthusiasts seek out the 1840 Warner-Waterloo Bridge, west of town on Newmarket Road, and the 1853 Warner-Dalton Bridge, which crosses over the Warner River. Contoocook, one of Hopkinton's three villages, has the oldest railroad covered bridge in the United States.

DIRECTIONS FOR THE RIDE

The ride begins in the parking lot at the junction of NH 103 and West Main Street in Bradford. There is a market here that sells food and drinks.

0.0 From West Main Street, turn left at the traffic light, heading east on NH 103.

0.5 Side trip: Turn right onto Center Road for a look at Bement Bridge, a covered bridge crossing the West Branch of the Warner River. It was built in 1854 for five hundred dollars.

0.7 At the traffic light, turn right onto NH 114, following the sign to Henniker. *This leg of the tour is a series of long, gradual climbs and descents; you'll also ride along the long shoreline of Lake Massasecum.*

9.2 Cross US 202/NH 9 and begin the descent into Henniker.

9.8 Turn left onto Main Street.
New England College is the centerpiece of this village, but it also has a historic covered bridge, an art gallery, a handful of eateries, and a pharmacy that stocks an eclectic selection of goods, from fishing gear to wine.

10.0 At the end of Main Street, bear left onto Crescent Road.
This quiet country road turns into Old Concord Road as it parallels US 202. You'll pass a gravel pit and lumberyard, so expect some commercial truck traffic.

13.6 At the blinking traffic light, cross US 202/NH 9 onto NH 127.
Use caution crossing this very busy highway.

14.3 Follow NH 127 to the right as it crosses the Hopkinton Dam.

The Merrimack Valley in central New Hampshire is dotted with farmland and historic villages.

14.7 At the Hopkinton-Rowell Bridge, follow NH 127 as it turns to the right.
This 1853 covered bridge spans the Contoocook River.

18.0 Pass through the small village of Contoocook.
The covered bridge at Fountain Square, the Hopkinton Bridge, is out of service, but is considered the country's oldest railroad covered bridge.

18.5 At the stop sign, turn left onto NH 127/103, heading toward Warner.
There are a couple of markets here for supplies.

19.6 Pass the Hopkinton State Fairgrounds.
The annual country fair is held on Labor Day weekend.

20.6 At the general store in Davis, bear left onto NH 103.
This rural country road heading west toward Warner is dotted with nurseries, farms, and even a couple of cafés. The flat terrain is mixed with some rolling hills.

25.7 Pass through the historic village of Warner.
The Foothills Restaurant on Main Street is a local landmark, popular with the breakfast crowd.

34.0 At the traffic light, continue straight on NH 103.

34.4 At the next traffic light, turn right onto West Main Street in Bradford to end the ride.

Bicycle Shops

Outspokin' Bicycle & Sport Shop, NH 103 and 103A, Newbury; 603-763-9500; www.outspokin.com

Bob Skinner's Ski and Sports, NH 103, Newbury; 603-763-2303

Banagan's Cycling Company, 67 South Main Street, Concord; 603-225-3330; www.banagans.com

THE
CONNECTICUT
RIVER VALLEY

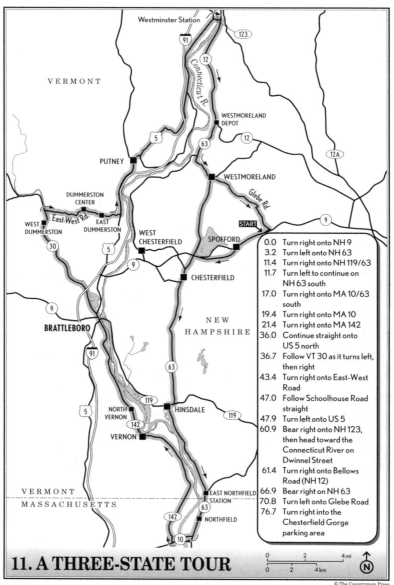

Westminster Station

VERMONT

PUTNEY

DUMMERSTON
CENTER

WEST
DUMMERSTON

East-West Rd.

EAST
DUMMERSTON

WEST
CHESTERFIELD

SPOFFORD

START

WESTMORELAND
DEPOT

WESTMORELAND

Glebe Rd.

Connecticut R.

NEW
HAMPSHIRE

CHESTERFIELD

BRATTLEBORO

NORTH
VERNON

HINSDALE

VERNON

VERMONT
MASSACHUSETTS

EAST NORTHFIELD
STATION

NORTHFIELD

Mile	Direction
0.0	Turn right onto NH 9
3.2	Turn left onto NH 63
11.4	Turn right onto NH 119/63
11.7	Turn left to continue on NH 63 south
17.0	Turn right onto MA 10/63 south
19.4	Turn right onto MA 10
21.4	Turn right onto MA 142
36.0	Continue straight onto US 5 north
36.7	Follow VT 30 as it turns left, then right
43.4	Turn right onto East-West Road
47.0	Follow Schoolhouse Road straight
47.9	Turn left onto US 5
60.9	Bear right onto NH 123, then head toward the Connecticut River on Dwinnel Street
61.4	Turn right onto Bellows Road (NH 12)
66.9	Bear right on NH 63
70.8	Turn left onto Glebe Road
76.7	Turn right into the Chesterfield Gorge parking area

11. A THREE-STATE TOUR

0   2   4 mi
0   2   4 km

N

New Hampshire–Massachusetts–Vermont: A Three-State Tour

- **DISTANCE:** 76.7 miles
- **TERRAIN:** Rolling to steep hills mixed with flat roads
- **DIFFICULTY:** Very strenuous
- **RECOMMENDED BICYCLE:** Touring/road bike

This tour explores a diverse collection of large and small Connecticut River valley towns in three states—New Hampshire, Massachusetts, and Vermont. It could be tackled as a challenging daylong tour or turned into two or three moderate days. (Lodging options along the way are listed at the end of the chapter.)

Back roads roll through picturesque farmland surrounding classic New England villages. Among these are Chesterfield, Hinsdale, and Westmoreland in New Hampshire. In Massachusetts, the only town you'll ride through is Northfield, which has the geographic distinction of being cut in two by the Connecticut River. In Vermont, you'll tour the city of Brattleboro, the village of Putney, and the barely-there hamlets of Vernon and Dummerston. Farms, produce stands, nurseries, and sugarhouses line the rural roads in between.

Brattleboro is a lively cultural hub, calling itself "All of Vermont, close to home." True to its word, this funky town offers the visitor a little of everything. It's worth a stop, if only to sample from its eclectic mix of cuisine, from Russian and Korean to vegan and traditional New England. Shops sell antiques, books, upscale clothing, and natural foods. Most of these fill remodeled and restored historic brick buildings downtown. Musical and theatrical performances and a thriving community of local artists and their studios and galleries round out Brattleboro's cultural offerings.

Farther along is Putney, a village at once historic and progressive, with an assortment of eateries, general stores, inns, artisans, private schools, and community events. The outskirts have been farmed for centuries, and many working farms remain.

You'll cross the West River on the Creamery Bridge, Vermont's longest covered bridge still in use, then head up into the hills to Dummerston Center, a pretty New England village that time passed by. After returning to the river valley, you'll cross the Connecticut once again and return to New Hampshire.

DIRECTIONS FOR THE RIDE

The ride begins at the Chesterfield Gorge State Wayside Parking Area on NH 9, just east of Spofford Lake, about 6 miles west of Keene. There are bathrooms and telephones at this trailhead to Chesterfield Gorge, and supplies can be picked up in Keene or at any of the towns on the tour.

0.0 Turn right out of the parking area, heading west on NH 9.
This is a major east-west highway, but the shoulder is wide and you will turn off the road soon.

3.2 Turn left onto NH 63, heading south toward Chesterfield.
Use caution crossing this busy highway.

4.2 Pass through the village of Chesterfield.
Chesterfield is perched on a ridge high in the hills above the Connecticut River valley. Leaving the village, you'll tackle a series of long climbs and descents on this rural road before a long descent into Hinsdale. Enjoy the wide-open views of meadow-covered hills backed by the rugged mountains of the Pisgah Range.

11.4 At the stop sign, turn right onto NH 119/63, following the sign to Brattleboro.
The historic town of Hinsdale has cafés and grocery stores where you can pick up supplies.

11.7 Turn left to continue on NH 63 south, crossing the Ashuelot River.
This winding country road will take you past a general store and through a wide farming valley along the Connecticut River.

16.3 Cross into Massachusetts and the town of Northfield.

17.0 At the stop sign, turn right onto MA 10/63 south, following signs for Greenfield and Northfield.

18.4 Pass through the village of Northfield.
Northfield is truly a Connecticut River town—it's the only town on this tour for which the river is not a boundary, but a part of the landscape. The grand historic homes along Main Street are a testament to the prosperity this community enjoyed from farming and river commerce.

19.4 Turn right onto MA 10, following signs to Greenfield and Bernardstown.
Shortly you'll cross the Connecticut River and climb for about a mile.

21.4 Turn right onto MA 142, following the signs to Brattleboro and Vernon, Vermont.
You'll ride toward the mountains in this long farming valley that follows the river and stays flat for the next 10 miles as you head north into Vermont.

A rural stretch of the Connecticut River between New Hampshire and Vermont

25.3 Cross into Vernon, Vermont.
On the outskirts of the village is the Vernon Historical Museum, which is housed in a tiny brick roadside building and open on Sundays. A grocery store is located a couple of miles north.

30.5 Pass through the center of Vernon.
Vernon is a quiet agricultural town surrounded by cornfields and farm stands.

34.9 Enter the outskirts of Brattleboro.
You'll pass by the sprawling riverfront warehouses and lumberyards that mark the southern fringes of downtown Brattleboro.

36.0 At the stop sign in downtown Brattleboro, continue straight onto US 5 north.
Use caution riding through the city's busy streets. Be sure to stop in at Brattleboro Bicycle Shop on Main Street.

36.7 Follow VT 30 as it turns left, then right.
Once you leave Brattleboro, the rural scenery returns on this country road as it follows the winding West River into Dummerston, with the New Hampshire mountains marching past on the eastern horizon.

42.7 There is a grocery store/deli in West Dummerston for food and supplies.

43.4 Turn right onto East-West Road, crossing the West River on the Creamery Bridge, Vermont's longest covered bridge still in use.
This is the route's biggest challenge, a grinding 2-mile climb through thick woods to the picturesque hilltop hamlet of Dummerston Center.

45.9 At the stop sign in Dummerston Center, continue straight (past the white clapboard grange hall) to begin the 2-mile descent to East Dummerston.
Enjoy the well-deserved descent, but use caution. There are many sharp turns, and the road winds all the way down.

47.0 At the fork in the road in East Dummerston, follow Schoolhouse Road straight (East-West Road continues to the right).

47.9 At the stop sign, turn left onto US 5.
This rolling road heads north toward Putney.

50.6 Pass through the village of Putney.

Among the many places to stop for a bite are the Putney Food Co-op, Putney General Store, and the Putney Diner. There is also an impressive group of resident artisans and craftspeople. Studios and galleries throughout town showcase work in furniture making, weaving, glassblowing, and pottery.

54.1 Pass Harlow's Sugar House and Santa's Land USA.
In the unlikely event you're accompanied by small children during this ride, see the Christmas theme village; otherwise, stop by the sugarhouse, where you can take a tour during sugaring season. Or just enjoy the ride through rural farmland.

60.9 At Westminster Station, bear right onto NH 123.
Ride beneath the underpass and head toward the Connecticut River on Dwinnel Street.

61.4 Cross the river to return to New Hampshire, then turn right onto Bellows Road (NH 12) and head south toward Walpole.
This road is busy, but has a wide shoulder to ride on.

66.9 Bear right onto NH 63.

69.2 Ascend a short, steep hill into the village of Park Hill.
The gleaming white Park Hill Meetinghouse sits at the side of the road, marking the beginning of a long, winding descent toward Westmoreland.

70.8 In front of the Westmoreland Village Store, turn left onto Glebe Road.
This woods road climbs and dips for the tour's last 5 miles.

75.6 Continue straight when the road parallels NH 9.

76.7 The ride ends with a right turn into the Chesterfield Gorge parking area.

Bicycle Shops

Banagan's Cycling Company, 82 Main Street, Keene, NH; 603-357-2331; www.banagans.com

Brattleboro Bicycle Shop, 178 Main Street, Brattleboro, VT; 802-254-8644; 1-800-BRATBIKE; www.bratbike.com

West Hill Shop, 49 Brickyard Lane, Putney, VT; 802-387-5718; www.westhillshop.com

Lodging

Chesterfield Inn, NH 9 (P.O. Box 155), West Chesterfield, NH 03466; 603-256-3211; 1-800-365-5515

Centennial House, 94 Main Street, Northfield, MA 01360; 413-498-5921; 1-877-977-5950

40 Putney Road, 40 Putney Road, Brattleboro, VT 05301; 802-254-6268; 1-800-941-2413

Hickory Ridge House, RFD 3 (P.O. Box 1410), Putney, VT 05346; 802-387-5709; 1-800-380-9218

The Walpole Inn, 297 Main Street (P.O. Box 762), Walpole, NH 03608; 603-756-3320

Windsor, Vermont, via the Cornish-Windsor Covered Bridge

- **DISTANCE:** 11.3 miles
- **TERRAIN:** Flat and gently rolling
- **DIFFICULTY:** Easy
- **RECOMMENDED BICYCLE:** Touring/road bike

This quick jaunt up and down Vermont and New Hampshire's Upper Valley region is highlighted by a trip across the Connecticut River on the 1866 Cornish-Windsor Bridge, the longest covered wooden bridge in the United States. A painted sign remains that advised long-ago bridge users to "Walk your horses or pay two dollars fine."

In both states, this is a community of working farms, with corn-fields spread along the fertile riverbanks and herds of dairy cows grazing in green meadows, all backed by the foothills of steep mountain ranges. There are only two small river towns on this ride—Ascutney and Windsor—and they're both in Vermont. New Hampshire offers several miles of uninterrupted farmland in Cornish, from the covered bridge to the outskirts of Claremont, as well as a spectacular view of Vermont's Mount Ascutney looming large over the river.

In the early 20th century, Cornish was a popular writers' and artists' colony, attracting such recognized artists as the sculptor Augustus Saint-Gaudens, whose hilltop estate is open to the public, and the painter Maxfield Parrish, whose work fills a local museum (see Ride 13: The Cornish Colony).

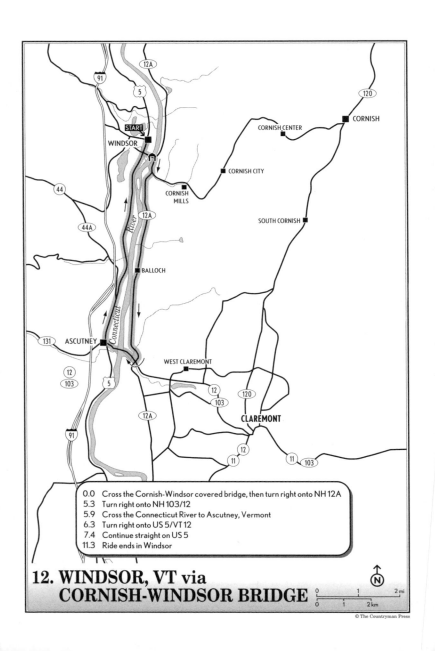

0.0	Cross the Cornish-Windsor covered bridge, then turn right onto NH 12A
5.3	Turn right onto NH 103/12
5.9	Cross the Connecticut River to Ascutney, Vermont
6.3	Turn right onto US 5/VT 12
7.4	Continue straight on US 5
11.3	Ride ends in Windsor

12. WINDSOR, VT via
CORNISH-WINDSOR BRIDGE

© The Countryman Press

Windsor was a thriving industrial town in the mid-19th century, with brick mills producing everything from rifles to paper. The American Precision Museum, housed in a historic four-story brick armory, has tool and manufacturing exhibits. Other vintage buildings still stand in town, most notably the Windsor House, the 1798 Old South Congregational Church, and a collection of handsome mansions, lasting reminders of this river town's prosperity.

Perhaps more historically significant, Windsor is regarded as the "birthplace of Vermont." At a tavern here in the summer of 1777, Vermont was declared an independent state, separated from New Hampshire by the Connecticut River. The official state line runs along the Vermont side of the river, leaving New Hampshire with the responsibility of maintaining the covered bridges that link the two states up and down the long border. The Old Constitution House, where the new state's constitution was adopted, is now a local history museum on North Main Street.

Ascutney is connected to Windsor by US 5, an old river highway that has been eclipsed by I-91. Most visitors come here to hike or ski 3,144-foot Mount Ascutney, the highest peak in the Connecticut River valley, which rises dramatically from the valley floor.

DIRECTIONS FOR THE RIDE

The ride starts in Windsor, Vermont. There is plenty of street parking, as well as a small public lot on Railroad Avenue, just off Main Street.

0.0 Cross the Cornish-Windsor Covered Bridge to New Hampshire, then turn right onto NH 12A.
The terrain is refreshingly flat and gently rolling, with miles of cornfields. Views of Mt. Ascutney, dairy farms, produce stands, silos, barns, and nurseries punctuate the scenery as you head south toward Claremont.

0.3 The Dingleton Hill Covered Bridge is a short distance to the left down Town House Road.
Local builder James Tasker constructed this bridge over Mill Brook in 1882.

5.3 At the traffic light, turn right onto NH 103/12.
This road is busy, but has a wide shoulder to ride on.

The gentle terrain in the Connecticut River valley is popular with cyclists.

5.9 Cross the Connecticut River to Ascutney, Vermont.

6.3 At the traffic light on the opposite bank, turn right onto US 5/VT 12. *Most people travel to Ascutney to ski Ascutney Mountain Resort, a popular family vacation destination. The Ascutney Market has groceries and supplies.*

7.4 At the junction of VT 44, continue straight on US 5.

11.3 The ride ends in Windsor.

Bicycle Shops

Banagan's Cycling Company, 187 Mechanic Street, Lebanon; 603-448-5556; www.banagans.com

Claremont Cyclesport, 51 Pleasant Street, Claremont; 603-542-2453; 1-800-831-2453; www.cyclesport.com

13

The Cornish Colony

- **DISTANCE:** 23 miles
- **TERRAIN:** Flat roads mixed with rolling hills
- **DIFFICULTY:** Moderate
- **RECOMMENDED BICYCLE:** Touring/road bike

The agricultural river town of Cornish blossomed into a thriving art colony in the early 1900s, when artists and writers began summering in the rural countryside along the Connecticut River. When farming began to decline in the valley, many artists settled permanently in the old farmhouses. They became known as the Cornish Colony, a creative group of painters, illustrators, and novelists drawing inspiration from the beauty of their surroundings. Among them was Maxwell Parrish, whose paintings are on display at the Cornish Colony Gallery and Museum, the writer Winston Churchill, and artist Ellen Wilson, wife of President Woodrow Wilson, who summered at Churchill's home in 1914 and 1915 (look for the historical marker by the Cornish-Windsor Bridge for more on Churchill).

Many of these transplanted artists were friends of the prominent sculptor Augustus Saint-Gaudens, whose 150-acre hilltop mansion, Aspet, is now a national historic park overlooking the river. In the late 19th century, the estate served as the social hub for the Cornish Colony. Today, visitors can view his work in the studio, gallery, and sculpture court. The work of Saint-Gaudens's contemporaries is on display at the above-mentioned art museum, a

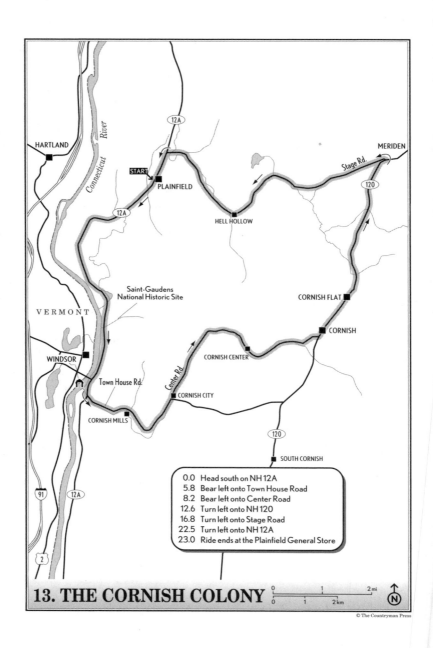

HARTLAND

Connecticut River

12A

MERIDEN

Stage Rd.

START

PLAINFIELD

12A

HELL HOLLOW

120

Saint-Gaudens
National Historic Site

CORNISH FLAT

VERMONT

CORNISH

WINDSOR

Town House Rd.

Center Rd.

CORNISH CENTER

CORNISH CITY

CORNISH MILLS

120

SOUTH CORNISH

91

12A

2

0.0   Head south on NH 12A
5.8   Bear left onto Town House Road
8.2   Bear left onto Center Road
12.6 Turn left onto NH 120
16.8 Turn left onto Stage Road
22.5 Turn left onto NH 12A
23.0 Ride ends at the Plainfield General Store

13. THE CORNISH COLONY

0   1   2 mi
0   1   2 km

N

© The Countryman Press

former country estate just down the road from Aspet. The museum is noted for its extensive collection of Maxwell Parrish paintings, the largest such exhibit in the country.

The most recognized landmark in this area is the Cornish-Windsor Bridge, built on a bend in the Connecticut River in 1866 by local resident James Tasker. Its impressive 450-foot span makes it the longest historic covered bridge in the country. With Mount Ascutney towering above the Vermont side of the river, the bridge is a frequently photographed and painted icon of the past. Three other 19th-century covered bridges—Blow-Me-Down, Blacksmith Shop, and Dingleton Hill—are on or near this ride and worth a look.

The ride begins in the tiny village of Plainfield, established in 1761. The town hall has been standing since 1798; the general store since 1858. The illustrator Maxwell Parrish, perhaps Plainfield's most famous resident, now has the stretch of NH 12 through town named in his honor. A stage set he designed in 1916 is periodically on display at the town hall. Actress Ethel Barrymore was among the stars who summered here.

A historical side note: The origin of the unusual name "Blow-Me-Down"—which refers collectively to a mill, a grange hall, a hiking trail, and a covered bridge—is a stream that flows through the outskirts of Cornish, called Blomidon. That name evolved into Blow-Me-Down, which is what the stream is called today.

DIRECTIONS FOR THE RIDE

The ride begins on NH 12 at the general store in Plainfield. The wide front porch is an inviting place to enjoy lunch or ice cream after the ride.

0.0 From the Plainfield General Store, head south on NH 12A.
The landscape of cornfields and wide-open farmland speckled with barns and silos is a hallmark of this tour, as well as the entire river valley between Vermont and New Hampshire. Mount Ascutney across the river provides a dramatic backdrop.

1.4 To the left on Mill Road is Blow-Me-Down Bridge.
This covered bridge was built in the 1880s over Blow-Me-Down Brook.

The rural countryside in Cornish attracted many artists and writers in the 19th century.

2.4 The yellow clapboard house on the right is the Cornish Colony Gallery & Museum.
This nonprofit museum, at the former Mastlands estate, is open from late-May to mid-October.

3.7 Pass Blow-Me-Down Mill.
A historical marker at the site explains the background of the Cornish Colony–era artists and writers who settled here from 1883–1935.

3.9 Pass the entrance to the Saint-Gaudens National Historic Site.
The approach to the hilltop mansion is a muscle-burning climb, but if you're so inclined, the house and grounds are open May through October, daily 9–4:30.

5.4 The Cornish-Windsor Covered Bridge crosses to Windsor, Vermont.
The bridge isn't part of the route, but you'd be remiss not to take a quick spin across to the Vermont side and back.

5.8 At the yield sign by the small grocery store, bear left onto Town House Road.
This narrow, winding road leads up into the woods.

6.6 Pass by the Dingleton Hill Covered Bridge at the junction of Root Hill Road.

7.8 Pass the Blacksmith Shop Covered Bridge, a weathered brown structure set off the road.

8.2 Bear left onto Center Road.
A few homes and horse pastures are scattered along this isolated country byway that cuts through a gentle valley.

12.6 At the stop sign, turn left onto NH 120, heading north toward Cornish.

13.6 The village of Cornish has a general store at a small green where you can stop for supplies.
From here, the road cuts through a long farming valley before climbing to hilltop farmland.

16.8 Turn left onto Stage Road.
This rural road leads west toward the Connecticut River through several miles of quiet woodland.

22.5 Turn left onto NH 12A.
Now you're riding south toward Plainfield.

23.0 The ride ends at the Plainfield General Store.

Bicycle Shops

Banagan's Cycling Company, 187 Mechanic Street, Lebanon; 603-448-5556; www.banagans.com

Claremont Cyclesport, 51 Pleasant Street, Claremont; 603-542-2453; 1-800-831-2453; www.cyclesport.com

Dartmouth Outdoor Rentals, Robinson Hall, on the Dartmouth green, Hanover; 603-646-1747

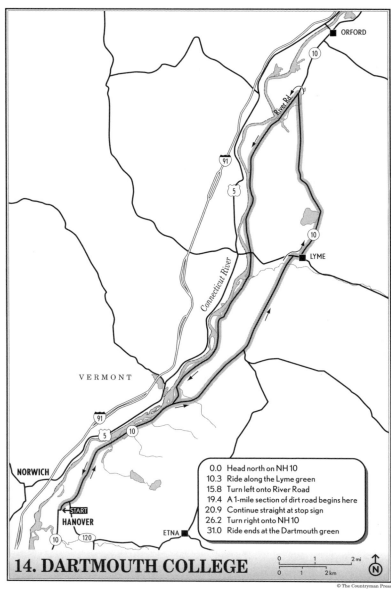

ORFORD

10

River Rd.

91

5

10

LYME

Connecticut River

VERMONT

91

5

10

NORWICH

0.0   Head north on NH 10
10.3 Ride along the Lyme green
15.8 Turn left onto River Road
19.4 A 1-mile section of dirt road begins here
20.9 Continue straight at stop sign
26.2 Turn right onto NH 10
31.0 Ride ends at the Dartmouth green

←START
HANOVER

ETNA

10   120

14. DARTMOUTH COLLEGE

0   1   2 mi
0   1   2 km

N

© The Countryman Press

Dartmouth College

- **DISTANCE:** 31 miles
- **TERRAIN:** Flat stretches mixed with rolling terrain; a 1-mile section of hard-packed dirt road
- **DIFFICULTY:** Moderate
- **RECOMMENDED BICYCLE:** Touring/road bike

Chartered in 1769 for the education of "youth of the Indian Tribes...English youth and others," Dartmouth College is a historic icon along the Connecticut River, not to mention one of the nation's most prestigious Ivy League institutions.

The campus, as well as the eclectic-yet-homey New England college town of Hanover, is a lively cultural center for much of the Upper Valley region, and well worth exploring after the ride. Wine bars, bistros, coffeehouses, and restaurants, serving everything from gourmet New England fare to Thai cuisine, cater to townsfolk, visiting gourmands, and more than five thousand college students. During the academic year, there is a full schedule of university-staged theatrical and creative arts performances, student shows and exhibits, and film society movie screenings.

The gently rolling country roads north of Dartmouth lead to Lyme, a quaint village surrounded by cornfields, horse pastures, and open meadows dotted with silos and barns. The green is surrounded by historic gems, including the white clapboard Lyme Country Store; two charming inns, one housed in an 1809 tavern; and the 1812 Federal-style Congregational church, with its rambling horse shed complete with 27 named and numbered stalls, reserved for churchgoers of centuries past.

You'll return to Hanover on River Road, the kind of old-time back road that's a cyclist's dream. The broad plain above the eastern side of the Connecticut River is a patchwork of working farmland, and much of the surrounding woodland is protected as a wildlife conservation area. This wide and slow stretch of water is popular with canoeists and kayakers. You might even spot a Dartmouth crew or a single sculler gliding along, especially in the early morning hours when the mirror/like surface makes for the best rowing.

The leafy, elm-shaded Dartmouth green marks both the start of this ride and the heart of this historic campus. Take note of the handsome brick Baker Library, modeled after Philadelphia's Independence Hall, and the austere 18th-century Hanover Inn on the opposite end of the green. For a closer look at the university, take one of the campus tours that leave daily from the white information kiosk.

DIRECTIONS FOR THE RIDE

The ride begins on the Dartmouth green at the white information kiosk on College Street. There are public parking lots in town, just south of the green, as well as stores where you can pick up supplies.

0.0 From the green, head north on NH 10.
Once you leave campus, you'll head downhill into mostly flat, open terrain. The Connecticut River shows itself in a couple of miles, then a string of farm fields signals your approach into the village of Lyme.

10.3 Ride along the Lyme green.
A row of quaint buildings, including a bed & breakfast and the Lyme Country Store, line the road. At the Congregational church, check out the shed where townsfolk would leave their mounts during Sunday services in the days of horse-drawn carriages. The family names remain above each stall.

10.6 At the end of the green, continue north on NH 10.
You'll ride past several miles of farmland, horses pastures, and cornfields before crossing into the outskirts of Orford.

A country road along the Connecticut River

15.8 Turn left onto River Road.
This gently rolling, lightly traveled country road cuts through cornfields, woods, and sprawling farmland for nearly 3 miles before the Connecticut River comes into view. Enjoy the peaceful surroundings and rewarding scenery. You can even catch glimpses of Vermont farms lining the western bank of the river.

16.7 Pass the weathered gray Edgell Covered Bridge over Clay Brook.

19.4 A 1-mile section of hard-packed dirt road begins here.

20.9 At the stop sign, continue straight.
The metal bridge to the right crosses the river to the rural village of East Thetford, Vermont.

26.2 At the stop sign, turn right onto NH 10.
This road will make you feel as if you've reentered civilization. Follow it south to return to Hanover.

31.0 The ride ends at the Dartmouth green.

Bicycle Shops

Dartmouth Outdoor Rentals, Robinson Hall, on the Dartmouth green, Hanover; 603-646-1747

Banagan's Cycling Company, 187 Mechanic Street, Lebanon; 603-448-5556; www.banagans.com

15

River Villages

- **DISTANCE:** 41.1 miles
- **TERRAIN:** Long, flat stretches along the Connecticut River mixed with rolling hills
- **DIFFICULTY:** Moderate to strenuous
- **RECOMMENDED BICYCLE:** Touring/road bike

The Upper Connecticut River valley is unique in that it combines two states—Vermont and New Hampshire—into one recognized geographic region. Both states contribute a fine collection of historic river villages, each surrounded by picture-postcard farmland dotted with barns and silos, meadows and forest. The result is one of the most idyllic and scenic regions in all of New England.

The ride begins in Woodsville, New Hampshire, a 19th-century railroad town with a historic rail station and a covered bridge that's believed to be the oldest in New England. You'll cross the Connecticut River into Wells River, Vermont, the starting point for touring the river's western side before exploring the New Hampshire communities on the eastern bank.

US 5 is an old Vermont river highway that follows the slow course of the Connecticut through two of the most stately villages in the Upper Valley. Newbury had a grand resort hotel here in the 19th century, when the town was famous for its mineral spa. Today the hotel is gone, but the elegant historic buildings along Main Street remain. The pretty town of Bradford sits above the river several miles downstream, with a friendly general store in a former

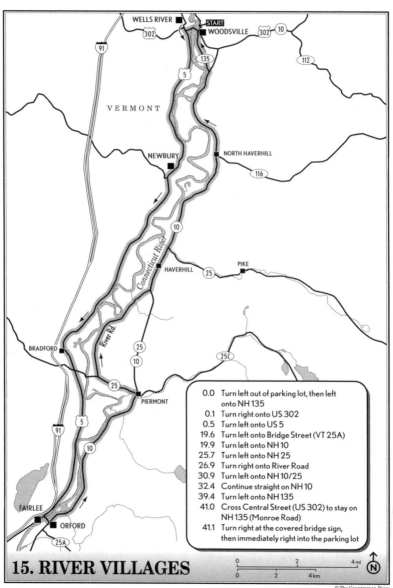

0.0	Turn left out of parking lot, then left onto NH 135
0.1	Turn right onto US 302
0.5	Turn left onto US 5
19.6	Turn left onto Bridge Street (VT 25A)
19.9	Turn left onto NH 10
25.7	Turn left onto NH 25
26.9	Turn right onto River Road
30.9	Turn left onto NH 10/25
32.4	Continue straight on NH 10
39.4	Turn left onto NH 135
41.0	Cross Central Street (US 302) to stay on NH 135 (Monroe Road)
41.1	Turn right at the covered bridge sign, then immediately right into the parking lot

15. RIVER VILLAGES

0   2   4 mi
0   2   4 km

N

19th-century hotel and an impressive assortment of quality eateries, unusual for such a small community.

The last stop on the Vermont side is Fairlee, a quaint one-street village on a bend of the Connecticut River with a classic 1930s diner and a 19th-century pharmacy. The palisades rising above the river are home to nesting migratory birds, including peregrine falcons. Dawn and dusk are the best times to see the birds diving from their nests on the cliffs.

You'll return to New Hampshire on a steel bridge that leads to the historic river town of Orford. Ridge Row is a stately lineup of seven Federal-style mansions built above Main Street from 1773 to 1839 for some of the area's wealthiest residents. The impressive architecture of these elegant homes is the work of local craftsmen of the era. Adding to the beauty of the Row are the long entrances lined with ancient oaks that lead to each estate. Across the street is the general store, serving townsfolk since 1804, and prim New England houses set behind white picket fences.

The hilltop villages of Piermont and Haverhill have the requisite New England commons with splendid vintage Federal-era buildings, symbols of the prosperous history of these centuries-old farming communities. The lofty farmland surrounding these historic centers is synonymous with the Upper Valley. Farm fields stretch to far-off peaks, over rolling hills dotted with barns, silos, and cornfields. The river stays in view most of the time, winding its way through this beautiful pastoral landscape.

Historians agree that the Connecticut River didn't so much divide New Hampshire and Vermont as unite them. The river once served as the main highway through this region, with steamboats plying goods and travelers back and forth well into the 1800s. Towns on both banks thrived, and many of their residents prospered and built elegant mansions and public buildings that still stand today. Perhaps the best-known resident of Orford's Ridge Row was Samuel Morey, who designed the nation's first paddle-wheeled steamboat and tested it on the river in 1793.

Moreover, many modern visitors to the Upper Valley discover that both sides of the Connecticut share a common identity; one state doesn't differ dramatically from the other. In fact, the region seems unified in character and setting. Residents here felt the same way in the 1770s, going as far as lobbying for the creation of "New Connecticut," a state made up of towns on both sides of the river. Their efforts were squashed by the creation of Vermont as an independent state in July 1777, with the signing of a constitution in Windsor, Vermont, a river town downstream (see Ride 12: Windsor, Vermont, via the Cornish-Windsor Covered Bridge).

DIRECTIONS FOR THE RIDE

The ride begins in Woodsville, New Hampshire. Parking is available in a small lot on NH 135 just north of the junction of US 302 in the center of town.

0.0 Turn left from the parking lot, then left again onto NH 135.

0.1 At the stop sign, turn right onto US 302, following the sign to Wells River, Vermont.
Follow the road downhill, beneath the underpass, and across the Connecticut River on a green steel bridge to Vermont.

0.5 At the stop sign, turn left onto US 5 in Wells River, heading south toward Newbury and Bradford, Vermont.

6.1 Pass through Newbury.

12.7 Ride through the village of Bradford.
This oft-photographed tableau of farmland, slow-flowing river, and distant mountain peaks is one of the prettiest landscapes in New England.

19.6 In Fairlee, turn left onto Bridge Street (VT 25A), following the sign for Orford, New Hampshire.
You must walk your bike over the green steel bridge using the pedestrian walkway.

19.9 At the stop sign, turn left onto NH 10, heading north along the Orford green.
The mansions of Ridge Row stand like sentries high above the long green. There's a well-stocked general store in Orford.

25.7 At the blinking traffic light in Piermont, turn left onto NH 25.
This white clapboard farming community sits high above the river. Use caution on the short, steep downhill leaving the village.

26.9 Turn right onto River Road.

You'll see more of the same stunning pastoral views and bucolic scenes. This quiet back road has more barns, horses, produce stands, and cornfields than houses. The road will gradually rise into the woods over a series of rolling hills as it pulls away from the river.

30.9 At the stop sign, turn left onto NH 10/25.

31.8 Ride through the rural town of Haverhill.

This Colonial settlement, established in 1763, is preserved much as it was in the 18th century and contains seven unique villages. The handsome vintage homes and regal public buildings along the green are lasting reminders of Haverhill's heyday, when it was the seat of Grafton County for nearly a century, beginning in 1773.

A centuries-old mansion along Ridge Row in Orford

32.3 Side trip to Bedell Bridge State Park.
About a mile down a dirt road that cuts through cornfields you'll find the remnants of a covered bridge that once spanned the river to South Newbury, Vermont. Today it's a peaceful spot for a picnic or quiet rest.

32.4 Continue straight on NH 10 where NH 25 turns to the right.

33.5 Pass the North Haverhill fairgrounds.
The annual country fair is held in early August.

36.2 At the junction of NH 116 in North Haverhill, continue north on NH 10.
You can pick up supplies at the Aldrich General Store.

39.4 Turn left onto NH 135, at the brown covered bridge sign.
Like many river-valley roads, this one passes through acres of cornfields. Among these fields, however, is a sight seldom seen amid farmland—a drive-in movie theater.

41.0 At the stop sign in Woodsville, cross Central Street (US 302) to stay on NH 135 (Monroe Road).

41.1 Turn right at the covered bridge sign, then take an immediate right into the parking lot to end the ride.
The 1829 Haverhill-Bath Covered Bridge, spanning the Ammonoosuc River, is past the railroad underpass on NH 135, just north of the town center. It's the state's oldest covered bridge still in use.

Bicycle Shops

Littleton Bike Shop, 87 Main Street (US 302), Littleton; 603-444-3437; www
.littletonbike.com

Banagan's Cycling Company, 187 Mechanic Street, Lebanon; 603-448-5556;
www.banagans.com

THE
LAKES REGION

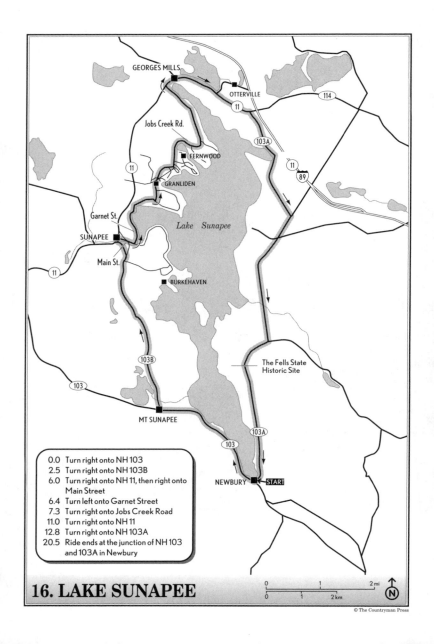

Jobs Creek Rd.

GEORGES MILLS

OTTERVILLE

114

11

103A

FERNWOOD

11

89

GRANLIDEN

Garnet St.

Lake Sunapee

SUNAPEE

Main St.

BURKEHAVEN

The Fells State
Historic Site

103B

103

103A

MT SUNAPEE

103

NEWBURY   START

0.0 Turn right onto NH 103
2.5 Turn right onto NH 103B
6.0 Turn right onto NH 11, then right onto
     Main Street
6.4 Turn left onto Garnet Street
7.3 Turn right onto Jobs Creek Road
11.0 Turn right onto NH 11
12.8 Turn right onto NH 103A
20.5 Ride ends at the junction of NH 103
      and 103A in Newbury

16. LAKE SUNAPEE

0   1   2 mi
0   1   2 km

N

Lake Sunapee

- **DISTANCE:** 20.5 miles
- **TERRAIN:** Rolling hills with a few steep climbs
- **DIFFICULTY:** Moderate to Strenuous
- **RECOMMENDED BICYCLE:** Touring/road bike

Lake Sunapee is perched over a thousand feet above sea level in a hilly area commonly referred to as the Western Lakes, southwest of Lake Winnipesaukee and east of the Connecticut River valley. It's a rolling landscape of picturesque farm fields and forests, dotted with sparkling lakes and ponds.

Riding along the lake affords countless views of glittery harbors, smart shoreline cottages, and boats of all kinds plying the clear waters. The lofty peak of Mount Sunapee on the southern shore stands sentinel over the route, attracting thousands of skiers in the winter and hikers during the rest of the year. This beautiful region lures its share of tourists, but it's refreshingly low-key compared to the bustling Lake Winnipesaukee area to the east. Locals take pride in Lake Sunapee for being one of New Hampshire's cleanest lakes.

The tour circles this long lake—10 miles north to south and only 3 miles wide. Many of the roads around the lake sit back from the shoreline, meandering close to the water in only a few spots. As a result, the hilly terrain surprises many cyclists new to the area. You'll enjoy plenty of water views riding along the western shore.

The summer crowds stroll quaint Sunapee, with its waterfront

A peaceful cove on the eastern shore of Lake Sunapee

galleries, cafés, and ice-cream shops. In the late 1800s, the harbor included several hotels, boarding houses, and a busy steamboat landing, from where tourists, arriving by train at Newbury Harbor, would be shuttled around the lake. The Sunapee Historical Society Museum, located in a former livery stable at the heart of the village, traces the history of this era through photographs and artifacts. Today, the grand hotels have been replaced by summer cottages and year-round homes. Visitors can leave the harbor on the steamer M/V *Kearsage* or the M/V *Mount Sunapee II* for an excursion around the lake. For a post-ride swim, head to Lake Sunapee State Park on the south shore in Newbury.

On the remote eastern shoreline is The Fells State Historic Site at the John Hay National Wildlife Refuge. The 42-room mansion and meticulously cared-for 20th-century perennial and woodland gardens are open to the public, and the 876-acre estate is laced with hiking trails. It's worth a stop to check out the Alpine Garden and the ancient stands of mountain laurel and rhododendron that bloom in profusion in late spring and early summer.

DIRECTIONS FOR THE RIDE

The ride starts at the dirt parking area across from Outspokin' Bicycle & Sport Shop, at the junction of NH 103 and 103A in Newbury. There is a market nearby selling food and drinks.

0.0 At the stop sign, turn right onto NH 103.
At the boat club you'll be treated to some fine lake views before embarking on a moderate rolling climb above the lake.

2.5 At the traffic rotary by Sunapee State Park, turn right onto NH 103B, heading north toward Sunapee.
The state park has picnicking areas as well as a 900-foot sand beach. This winding road continues to climb above the lake before descending into the village on Sunapee Harbor.

6.0 At the stop sign, turn right onto NH 11, cross a bridge, and then take an immediate right onto Main Street.
A short, steep hill takes you past the galleries and historic houses that line the narrow street leading toward picturesque Sunapee, whose bakery, ice-cream shop, cafés, and historical society museum make this a good stop.

6.4 Turn left onto Garnet Street.
This quiet side road winds above the lake past cottages that overlook the harbor.

7.3 At the stop sign, turn right onto Jobs Creek Road.
After a short, steep climb, this road rolls through the woods then dips down to Herrick Cove at the northern tip of the lake.

11.0 At the stop sign, turn right onto NH 11.
You can pick up supplies at the market in Georges Mills, then enjoy the views as you ride between the lake and Otter Pond.

12.8 Turn right onto NH 103A, just before the I-89 entrance ramp.
The road along the eastern shore is set into the hills and contains the route's most challenging terrain.

18.3 Pass the entrance for The Fells State Historic Site.
The former estate of diplomat John Hay sits high above the lakeshore. The grounds are open year-round; guided house tours are offered on summer weekends.

20.5 The ride ends at the junction of NH 103 and 103A in Newbury.

Bicycle Shops

Outspokin' Bicycle & Sport Shop, NH 103 and 103A, Newbury; 603-763-9500; www.outspokin.com

Bob Skinner's Ski and Sports, NH 103, Newbury; 603-763-2303

17

Enfield Shaker Village

- **DISTANCE:** 40.7 miles
- **TERRAIN:** Gently rolling to steep hills
- **DIFFICULTY:** Strenuous
- **RECOMMENDED BICYCLE:** Touring/road bike

The rural countryside north of Lake Sunapee offers miles of rolling back roads perfect for cycling. This tour starts near the top of the lake and winds north to Enfield, a quiet community blanketed in forest and spotted with lakes. It's also the site of a historic Shaker village, located along the western shore of Mascoma Lake.

The Enfield Shaker Museum in Lower Shaker Village tells the story of the community founded here in 1793. Like similar societies scattered across New England, its residents believed in the ideals of simplicity and practicality, putting their "hands to work and hearts to God." This thriving community resided along the lake throughout the height of the Shaker movement in the 1800s, practicing a communal lifestyle and unique type of worship. Today, the village is a museum, with workshops in Shaker crafts, gardening, and furniture making. Carefully restored buildings show the Shaker way of life, and a nearby gallery sells Shaker-design furniture and crafts, from wooden boxes to beds and armoires.

Aside from the scattered villages, most of this tour passes through remote natural areas. From the start near Little Sunapee Lake, you'll ride past fancy summer homes, then quiet and hilly land protected as state forest, as well as several wildlife management areas.

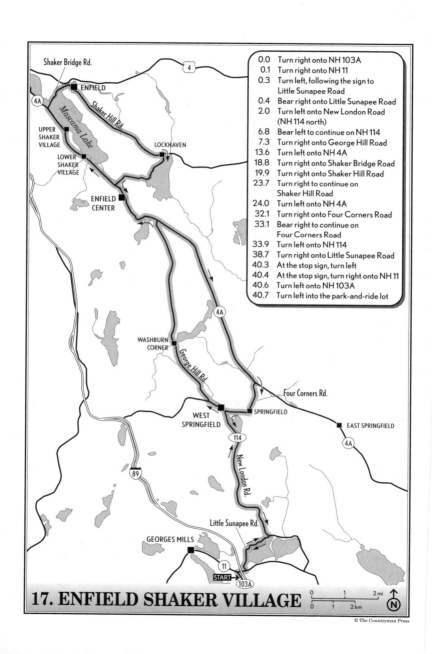

0.0	Turn right onto NH 103A
0.1	Turn right onto NH 11
0.3	Turn left, following the sign to Little Sunapee Road
0.4	Bear right onto Little Sunapee Road
2.0	Turn left onto New London Road (NH 114 north)
6.8	Bear left to continue on NH 114
7.3	Turn right onto George Hill Road
13.6	Turn left onto NH 4A
18.8	Turn right onto Shaker Bridge Road
19.9	Turn right onto Shaker Hill Road
23.7	Turn right to continue on Shaker Hill Road
24.0	Turn left onto NH 4A
32.1	Turn right onto Four Corners Road
33.1	Bear right to continue on Four Corners Road
33.9	Turn left onto NH 114
38.7	Turn right onto Little Sunapee Road
40.3	At the stop sign, turn left
40.4	At the stop sign, turn right onto NH 11
40.6	Turn left onto NH 103A
40.7	Turn left into the park-and-ride lot

17. ENFIELD SHAKER VILLAGE

© The Countryman Press

Be sure to carry bike supplies; the closest bike shops are in Newbury, at the southern tip of Lake Sunapee, and in Lebanon, near the northern part of the ride.

Enfield Center has a general store, historical society museum, and handsomely restored vintage homes surrounded by farms and cornfields.

DIRECTIONS FOR THE RIDE

The ride begins in New London at the commuter parking lot on NH 103A, at the junction of NH 11, near Exit 12 off I-89.

0.0 Turn right out of the parking lot onto NH 103A.

0.1 At the stop sign, turn right onto NH 11 and cross under I-89.

0.3 Turn left, following the sign to Little Sunapee Road.

0.4 Bear right onto Little Sunapee Road.
This quiet back road winds through the woods and hugs the shore of Little Sunapee Lake, which is lined with smart lake houses.

2.0 At the yield sign, turn left onto New London Road (NH 114 north).
This back road climbs and descends through the woods for 3 miles before following the western shore of Kolelemook Pond in Springfield.

6.8 At the junction of NH 4A in West Springfield, bear left to continue on NH 114.

7.3 Turn right onto George Hill Road.
Long climbs and descents roll past hilltop farms, deep woods, and distant mountain vistas.

13.6 At the stop sign, turn left onto NH 4A and pass George Pond.

14.8 Pass through Enfield Center.
Proctor's General Store, the historical society museum, and a collection of fine old homes front the road, then give way to gently rolling cornfields dotted with farmhouses, barns, and produce stands.

16.4 Ride along the western shore of Mascoma Lake.
Halfway up the lakeshore is Lower Shaker Village and its collection of more than a dozen buildings preserved as part of the Enfield Shaker Museum. One of them

A farm in the Lakes Region

has been converted into the Shaker Inn at the Great Stone Dwelling, a 19th-century four-story granite structure considered the largest existing Shaker dwelling. Guests stay in rooms furnished with the Shaker's trademark minimalist-designed beds, cabinets, and other pieces.

18.8 Turn right onto Shaker Bridge Road.
The road crosses a narrow causeway above the northern finger of the lake before passing through Enfield, where there is a small market.

19.9 Take the bridge over the Mascoma River, then turn right onto Shaker Hill Road.
The terrain is rural and rolling as you ride through the hills between Mascoma and Crystal Lakes.

23.7 At the stop sign, turn right (at the sign for Crystal Lake Road) to continue on Shaker Hill Road.

24.0 At the stop sign, turn left onto NH 4A.

32.1 Turn right onto Four Corners Road.

33.1 Bear right to continue on Four Corners Road.

33.9 At the stop sign in West Springfield, turn left onto NH 114.

38.7 Turn right onto Little Sunapee Road.

40.3 At the stop sign, turn left.

40.4 At the next stop sign, turn right onto NH 11.

40.6 Turn left onto NH 103A.

40.7 Turn left into the park-and-ride lot to end the ride.

Bicycle Shops

Outspokin' Bicycle & Sport Shop, NH 103 and 103A, Newbury; 603-763-9500; www.outspokin.com

Bob Skinner's Ski and Sports, NH 103, Newbury; 603-763-2303

Banagan's Cycling Company, 187 Mechanic Street, Lebanon; 603-448-5556; www.banagans.com

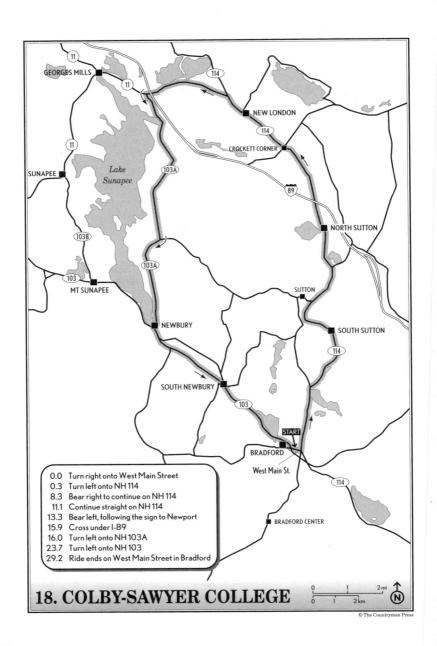

0.0 Turn right onto West Main Street
0.3 Turn left onto NH 114
8.3 Bear right to continue on NH 114
11.1 Continue straight on NH 114
13.3 Bear left, following the sign to Newport
15.9 Cross under I-89
16.0 Turn left onto NH 103A
23.7 Turn left onto NH 103
29.2 Ride ends on West Main Street in Bradford

18. COLBY-SAWYER COLLEGE

0   1   2 mi
0   1   2 km

N

© The Countryman Press

Colby-Sawyer College

- **DISTANCE:** 29.2 miles
- **TERRAIN:** Rolling hills
- **DIFFICULTY:** Moderate to Strenuous
- **RECOMMENDED BICYCLE:** Touring/road bike

New London is the commercial and cultural center of the western Lakes Region, due in large part to the presence of Colby-Sawyer College. This is small-town New England at its finest, with an 18th-century inn and historic campus buildings spread along a high ridge. The Barn Playhouse is home to one of the most highly regarded and oldest summer theaters in New England, and a restored collection of 19th-century village buildings is maintained by the local historical society and open to the public.

The Colby-Sawyer campus spreads across 80 acres in this hilltop town. The Marion Mugar Art Gallery has a full schedule of exhibits by renowned local artists, as well as faculty and students. Thanks to the presence of the college, New London has much to offer for a community its size—country inns, attractive shops, and excellent restaurants.

The ride begins in Bradford, a popular railroad-era stopover for visitors taking the train to Lake Sunapee. Next you'll pass through South Sutton, a historic mill village, and North Sutton, a tiny community on Kezar Lake. Each has a historic meetinghouse and general store. South Sutton has a museum stocked with local historical artifacts, while North Sutton used to have resort hotels on the lake.

Historic villages and country lanes surround New London.

The Follansbee Inn, on the main road through town, still welcomes overnight guests. The Lake Sunapee village of Newbury has an equal measure of country charm. The tour also passes a trio of lakes; the largest—Lake Sunapee—stays obscured by trees.

The countryside linking these places is rural and serene. Scattered along the way are pottery and crafts studios, orchards where you can pick your own apples and peaches, produce stands teeming with vegetables, even farms selling fresh bison steaks and burgers.

DIRECTIONS FOR THE RIDE

The ride begins in Bradford, at the junction of NH 103 and West Main Street. Park in the lot of the pizza restaurant, general store, and country store.

0.0 From the parking lot, turn right onto West Main Street.
The red clapboard Bowie's Market in Bradford is a good stop for food and supplies before or after the ride.

0.3 At the blinking traffic light, turn left onto NH 114.
This road climbs uphill before winding through the woods.

2.1 Ride past a cluster of cottages along the north shore of Blaisdell Lake.

4.3 Pass through the village of South Sutton.
Notice the historic general store (closed) and classic 1790s meetinghouse.

8.3 In North Sutton, bear right at the white clapboard meetinghouse and Vernondale's Country Store to continue on NH 114.
North Sutton used to have several large hotels on Kezar Lake. Today, the charming Follansbee Inn in the center of town takes in travelers.

11.1 At Crocket Corner, continue straight on NH 114 at the junction of NH 11, following the sign to New London.
A moderate mile-long climb to a high ridge will bring you to New London and Colby-Sawyer College.

12.2 Pass through New London.
This is a quintessential New England college town. Colby-Sawyer was founded here in 1837 as a small Baptist school. Today it's a four-year coed college spread across 80 hilltop acres.

13.3 At the blinking yellow traffic light, bear left, following the sign to Newport (NH 114 continues straight).
Ride through about a half-mile of commercial sprawl on the outskirts of New London.

15.9 Cross under I-89.

16.0 Turn left onto NH 103A.
This winding wooded road skirts the eastern shore of Lake Sunapee (there are no views of the lake from here) in a succession of climbs and descents.

23.7 At the stop sign in Newbury, turn left onto NH 103.
A bike shop and market are located at this intersection. Pass through the village of Newbury and its cluster of prim white buildings, then descend past Lake Todd on the way back to Bradford.

29.2 At the traffic light, turn left on West Main Street in Bradford to end the ride.

Bicycle Shops

Village Sports, 140 Main Street, New London; 603-526-4948

Outspokin' Bicycle & Sport Shop, NH 103 and 103A, Newbury; 603-763-9500; www.outspokin.com

Bob Skinner's Ski and Sports, NH 103, Newbury; 603-763-2303

Blackwater Ski Shop, 207 Main Street, Andover; 603-735-5437

19

Lake Winnipesaukee

- **DISTANCE:** 30 miles
- **TERRAIN:** Very hilly
- **DIFFICULTY:** Strenuous
- **RECOMMENDED BICYCLE:** Touring/road bike

Lake Winnipesaukee is something of an icon in New Hampshire and New England, and farther afield, as well. It is, after all, one of the nation's largest natural freshwater lakes, a 72-square-mile, spring-fed mountain oasis dotted with nearly three hundred islands.

Unfortunately for visitors, however, it may be one of the state's least accessible attractions. Most of the 283 miles of shoreline are privately owned; even most of the public beaches are restricted to locals and their guests. That's why the MS *Mount Washington* is a New Hampshire landmark. The 230-foot excursion boat runs spring to fall, giving thousands of visitors the best lake access there is.

This route explores the quiet side of the lake, far from the lively boardwalk and amusements (think water slides, mini golf, arcades, and go-carts) of bustling Weirs Beach, the mill town of Laconia, and the shopping centers of Tilton and Ashland, all on the western side. Instead, you'll tour peaceful hill towns like Moultonborough and Tuftonboro, farming communities whose centers are little more than a few tidy clapboard buildings, maybe a general store. While the western side of the lake is known for its exceptional views, the eastern shore offers a rural landscape that's rare for such a heavily

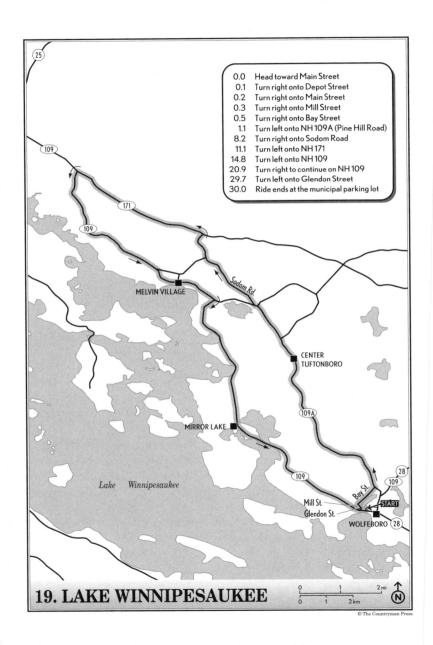

0.0	Head toward Main Street
0.1	Turn right onto Depot Street
0.2	Turn right onto Main Street
0.3	Turn right onto Mill Street
0.5	Turn right onto Bay Street
1.1	Turn left onto NH 109A (Pine Hill Road)
8.2	Turn right onto Sodom Road
11.1	Turn left onto NH 171
14.8	Turn left onto NH 109
20.9	Turn right to continue on NH 109
29.7	Turn left onto Glendon Street
30.0	Ride ends at the municipal parking lot

MELVIN VILLAGE

Sodom Rd.

CENTER TUFTONBORO

109A

MIRROR LAKE

Lake   Winnipesaukee

109

Bay St.

Mill St.

Glendon St.

START

WOLFEBORO   28

19. LAKE WINNIPESAUKEE

0   1   2 mi
0   1   2 km

N

touristed region.

The ride begins in Wolfeboro, a small-yet-upscale resort area known as the "Oldest Summer Resort in America." It's packed with the kind of attractive shops, museums, and quality restaurants you'd expect from a town with an exclusive prep school. Brewster Academy hosts the annual Great Waters Music Festival, a popular concert series on campus from July through September. On the way through town, you'll likely see many places that you'll want to come visit after the ride. Four such sites are museums, specializing in natural history, antique boats, World War II memorabilia, and two centuries of local artifacts.

Throughout the ride, especially in outlying wooded areas, mountain views appear frequently. Scattered old homes and historic settlements stand as tokens of the 19th century, when the eastern shoreline was mainly rolling farmland. This side of the lake remained so rural largely because the stagecoach and railroad lines exclusively served the western side.

Along the way you might want to check out Wolfeboro's Libby Museum, a 100-year-old natural history museum featuring exhibits, lectures, nature walks, and concerts. In Moultonborough, Castle in the Clouds is an early-20th-century estate sitting high above Lake Winnipesaukee on the flank of the Ossipee Mountains. Today, visitors can hike, picnic, ride horses, or tour the elegant stone mansion. Castle Springs water is bottled at its source here. Quaint Melvin village, tucked into a quiet bay, has a collection of antiques shops along its 19th-century Main Street.

Most climbs—and on this tour there are quite a few—seem to come with an immediate reward, a panoramic view of the lake or a string of lofty mountain peaks in the distance.

DIRECTIONS FOR THE RIDE

The tour begins in the center of Wolfeboro. Park in the municipal lot on Back Bay at the end of Glendon Street. Food, drinks, and bike supplies can be found in town.

0.0 Leave the parking area and head toward Main Street (NH 109).

0.1 Turn right onto Depot Street.

0.2 At the stop sign, turn right onto Main Street (NH 109).
As you ride through town, you can catch fleeting glimpses of the lake between the buildings.

0.3 Turn right onto Mill Street.

0.5 Turn right onto Bay Street.
Follow the bay past marinas and up a short hill through a quiet neighborhood.

1.1 At the stop sign, turn left onto NH 109A (Pine Hill Road).
Use caution riding on this narrow, winding road. There is a series of short, steep hills mixed with longer, more moderate climbs. This is wooded backcountry, laced with old stone walls that once marked the boundaries of meadows and farm fields.

6.2 Pass through the center of Tuftonboro.
This hilltop village has a general store.

8.2 Turn right onto Sodom Road.
This intersection is at the edge of a long field. Follow the narrow back road through the woods, up rollers that pass scattered homes and offer occasional glimpses of mountains through the trees.

11.1 At the stop sign, turn left onto NH 171.
Here the hills are longer but more gradual. Enter Moultonborough, a rural community of orchards, sugarhouses, and farms.

12.7 Pass the entrance to Castle Springs/Castle in the Clouds.
Farther down the road is the Castle Springs bottling plant, with tours available.

14.8 At the stop sign and blinking traffic light, turn left onto NH 109.
On the right are marinas and cottage roads, but the thick woods obstruct any lake views this far out.

19.8 Enjoy the first views of the lake as you ride through Melvin Village.
The Melvin Village General Store was for sale at the time of this writing.

20.9 Turn right onto NH 109, at the junction of NH 109A.
A steep climb ends with rewarding lake views. In a couple miles, the road descends all the way back to the edge of the lake, just before returning to the center of Wolfeboro.

25.1 Pass through Mirror Lake.

Lake Winnipesaukee's quiet eastern shore is hilly and rural.

This tiny hamlet is perched between two bodies of water, Mirror Lake and Winter Harbor.

26.4 Ride by the Libby Museum.
A local resident opened this natural history museum in 1912; today, it's maintained by the town of Wolfeboro and open during the summer months.

29.7 In the center of Wolfeboro, turn left onto Glendon Street.

30.0 The ride ends at the municipal parking lot.

Bicycle Shops

Wolfeboro Sports Outlet, 36 Glendon Street, Wolfeboro; 603-569-5777

Nordic Skier Sports, 47 North Main Street (NH 109), Wolfeboro; 603-569-3151

Mountain Sports, NH 3 and 106, Meredith; 603-279-5540

Ski Works, NH 16, West Ossipee; 603-539-2246

20

Squam Lake

- **DISTANCE:** 27.4 miles
- **TERRAIN:** Rolling and steep hills
- **DIFFICULTY:** Strenuous
- **RECOMMENDED BICYCLE:** Touring/road bike

Tucked a little northwest of Lake Winnipesaukee, Squam Lake is a wooded retreat. This remote and pristine lake, the second largest in New Hampshire, is small and quiet by Winnipesaukee standards. Here the waters are plied not by sailboats and cabin cruisers, but kayaks and canoes. It's known by movie audiences around the country as the setting of the classic *On Golden Pond*. Local tour operators are banking on the nostalgia, offering boat tours of the movie-filming location.

The ride begins at the northwestern tip of Lake Winnipesaukee in Center Harbor, a 19th-century village named for the prominent Senter family. The bronze goose fountain in the center of town was sculpted by S. G. Cook, a protégé of the noted sculptor Augustus Saint-Gaudens, who founded the Cornish Colony of artists and writers in the river valley town of Cornish. (See Ride 13: The Cornish Colony.)

Center Sandwich looks like a living New England postcard. The general store, gleaming white churches, and vintage homes clustered along the road make for an inviting stop. When pedaling the back roads of this sprawling hill town, keep in mind that in the late 1800s, this area virtually bustled with tourists

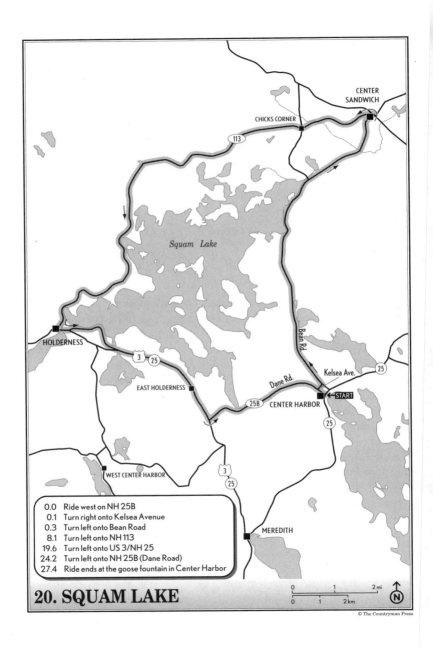

CENTER
SANDWICH

CHICKS CORNER

113

Squam Lake

HOLDERNESS

3 25

EAST HOLDERNESS

Dane Rd.

Bean Rd.

Kelsea Ave.

25

25B

CENTER HARBOR

START

25

WEST CENTER HARBOR

3
25

MEREDITH

0.0 Ride west on NH 25B
0.1 Turn right onto Kelsea Avenue
0.3 Turn left onto Bean Road
8.1 Turn left onto NH 113
19.6 Turn left onto US 3/NH 25
24.2 Turn left onto NH 25B (Dane Road)
27.4 Ride ends at the goose fountain in Center Harbor

0   1   2 mi
0   1   2 km

N

20. SQUAM LAKE

© The Countryman Press

who stayed on the dozens of farms that opened their doors to boarders.

The tiny waterfront village of Holderness is home to the Squam Lakes Natural Science Center, with its popular live animal programs and Golden Pond Boat Tours. As you'd expect from a town tucked between two bodies of water—Squam Lake and Little Squam Lake—many come here to kayak, canoe, and camp along the lakeshores.

Like many country roads, these have little or no shoulder to ride on. So ride defensively, and always be aware of your surroundings and the motorists sharing the road with you.

DIRECTIONS FOR THE RIDE

The ride begins at the fountain in Center Harbor. There is ample parking in town at Senter's Marketplace, the shopping complex where the E. M. Heath Supermarket is located.

0.0 From the fountain, ride west on NH 25B, past the library and away from the shore of Lake Winnipesaukee.

0.1 Turn right onto Kelsea Avenue.
This quiet neighborhood offers a shortcut that avoids the busy intersection in town.

0.3 At the stop sign, turn left onto Bean Road.
Be ready for some climbing; the road immediately heads into the high terrain above the lake.

3.2 Here the road meets the northeastern shore of Squam Lake.
You can see Kent Island, Hoag Island, and Long Point from here, as well as Otter Cove and Sandwich Bay. Look for birds and other wildlife in the marshes and quiet coves.

8.1 At the stop sign and blinking traffic light, turn left onto NH 113, following the sign to Holderness.
The long porch in front of the Sandwich General Store is cozy and inviting. It's another steep climb out of this picturesque village ringed with meadows and distant mountain views. Occasionally you'll spot a house, but mostly just long dirt driveways are visible from the road.

13.4 Cross into Holderness.

The outskirts of the Lakes Region remain largely agricultural.

You get the feeling that you're riding on high roads, even when the views are hidden by trees.

16.1 Ride along the western lakeshore.
Look at the house perched on its own tiny island just offshore.

19.4 Pass the Squam Lakes Natural Science Center.

19.6 At the stop sign, turn left onto US 3/NH 25.
If the center of Holderness appears surrounded by water, it basically is. A convenience store here sells food and drinks.

24.2 Turn left onto NH 25B (Dane Road).
After a climb, it's a long steep descent all the way back to Center Harbor. Enjoy the sweeping views of Lake Winnipesaukee on the way down, but use caution.

27.4 The ride ends at the goose fountain in Center Harbor.

Bicycle Shops

Mountain Sports, NH 3 and 106, Meredith; 603-279-5540

Rhino Bike Works, 95 South Main Street, Plymouth; 603-536-3919

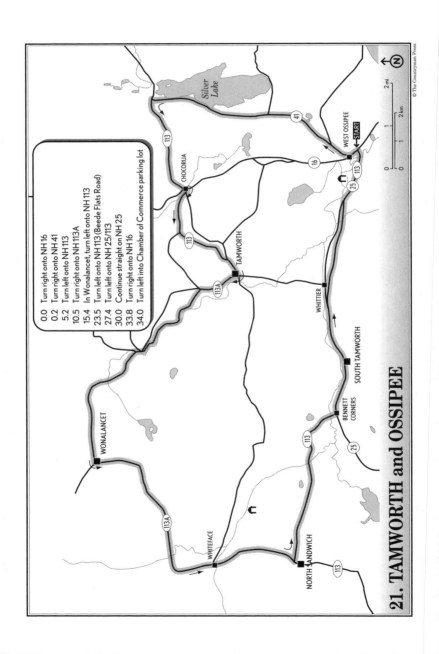

21. TAMWORTH and OSSIPEE

0.0	Turn right onto NH 16
0.2	Turn right onto NH 41
5.2	Turn left onto NH 113
10.5	Turn right onto NH 113A
15.4	In Wonalancet, turn left onto NH 113
23.5	Turn left onto NH 113 (Beede Flats Road)
27.4	Turn left onto NH 25/113
30.0	Continue straight on NH 25
33.8	Turn right onto NH 16
34.0	Turn left into Chamber of Commerce parking lot

Silver Lake

WEST OSSIPEE
START

CHOCORUA

TAMWORTH

WHITTIER

SOUTH TAMWORTH

BENNETT CORNERS

WONALANCET

WHITEFACE

NORTH SANDWICH

21

Tamworth and Ossipee

- **DISTANCE:** 34 miles
- **TERRAIN:** Rolling hills and flat stretches
- **DIFFICULTY:** Moderate
- **RECOMMENDED BICYCLE:** Touring/road bike

This rural, wooded area straddles the geographic line between central New Hampshire's rolling Lakes Region and the rugged White Mountains. As a result, the landscape is a softer blend of both regions. It's studded with small lakes and ponds and has hills that are steep enough to get your attention, although they don't measure up to the peaks up north. Since this area falls between the more popular tourist destinations, the back roads and surrounding landscape are blissfully quiet.

From West Ossipee, you'll head north past the shores of Silver Lake, then turn due west into Chocorua, known for the namesake peak that marks the southern fringe of the vast White Mountain National Forest. At 3,475 feet, Mount Chocorua is diminutive compared to its hulking neighbors, but it is popular with hikers because the bald summit offers the kind of views you usually have to climb much higher to achieve.

Tamworth is a sprawling 18th-century town encompassing seven villages; this tour passes through all but one. From Tamworth, with its charming inn, general store, and summer theater, you'll embark on an idyllic winding road that hugs the turns of the rushing Swift River. It traces the southern boundary of the Sandwich Range

Wilderness and Mount Chocorua Scenic Area, a vast mountainous tract packed with peaks, ridges, and ledges.

This scenic portion of Route 113A is also known as the Chinook Trail, and just past the village of Wonalancet the reason why will become clear. Farther on, the hamlets of North Sandwich and South Tamworth are sprinkled with hill farms and open meadows, many with centuries-old homesteads on their fringes. The League of New Hampshire Craftsmen, one of the nation's oldest statewide crafts organizations, was formed in Sandwich. Today it's based in Concord and represents local artists in galleries across the state.

DIRECTIONS FOR THE RIDE

Start at the parking area for the Greater Ossipee Area Chamber of Commerce, a small shuttered building in front of the West Ossipee post office, just south of the junction of NH 25 and NH 16.

0.0 Turn right out of the parking area onto NH 16.

0.2 Turn right onto NH 41, following the signs to Madison and Silver Lake. *This narrow, winding road cuts through a pine forest. An International Paper lumber mill is farther down the road.*

3.7 Pass the shore of Silver Lake.

5.2 At the stop sign, turn left onto NH 113, heading west toward Chocorua.

6.2 Cross into Tamworth.

7.6 At the stop sign and blinking traffic light, cross NH 16 and the Chocorua River, following the sign for NH 113. *This rural road into Tamworth is hilly and winding.*

10.5 At the blinking traffic light and stop sign, turn right onto NH 113A. *Tamworth has a small village center that time seems to have forgotten. Notice the Victorian inn, summer theater, library, and general store. From here, the road follows the winding course of the Swift River through dense woodland at the edge of the White Mountain National Forest.*

15.4 In tiny Wonalancet, turn left onto NH 113. *A little firehouse is the only indication that you've reached Wonalancet.*

15.9 Pass the site of the former Chinook Kennels.
Stop at the roadside slab of granite etched with the image of a dog sled. This is where Eva and Milton Seeley raised champion sled dogs—Alaskan malamutes and Siberian huskies that were used on dog teams for military operations, explorations, Army search and rescue units, and Admiral Byrd's famous expeditions to Antarctica. Today the property is a private residence.

16.9 Continue to follow NH 113A toward Sandwich, at the edge of a wide meadow.

18.2 Cross into Sandwich and enjoy this high, flat stretch of road.

21.9 Pass through the historic village of Whiteface.

23.5 At the stop sign, turn left onto NH 113 (Beede Flats Road), following the sign to Tamworth.

A common sight along New Hampshire's back roads

25.8 The Cold River Covered Bridge is located to the left, following the sign for Covered Bridge #45.

27.4 At the stop sign, turn left onto NH 25/113, heading east toward West Ossipee.
This busy, flat stretch of road follows the Bearcamp River. The South Tamworth Country Store about a mile ahead has food and drinks.

30.0 At the junction of NH 113, continue straight on NH 25.

33.3 The covered bridge at the end of Nudd Road is the Whittier Bridge, which spans the Bearcamp River (closed to traffic).

33.8 At the traffic light, turn right onto NH 16.

34.0 Turn left into the chamber of commerce parking lot to end the ride.

Bicycle Shops

Mountain Sports, NH 3 and 106, Meredith; 603-279-5540

Ski Works, NH 16, West Ossipee; 603-539-2246

Rhino Bike Works, 95 South Main Street, Plymouth; 603-536-3919

22

The Wakefield Lakes

- **DISTANCE:** 40.2 miles
- **TERRAIN:** Rolling hills and flat terrain
- **DIFFICULTY:** Moderate to Strenuous
- **RECOMMENDED BICYCLE:** Touring/road bike

Tucked along the far eastern edge of the Lakes Region is a rural expanse of forest and lakes, many of which straddle the border of New Hampshire and Maine. This tour stays in New Hampshire, except for a brief foray into Parsonfield, Maine, in order to negotiate the bulging shore of a lake.

The ride begins at the tip of Lovell Lake in Sanbornville, a village of Wakefield that thrived during the railroad era, when tracks were laid through town. Today it's quiet, with a couple of friendly eateries that lure visitors.

The road out of town, NH 153, is a state-designated scenic and cultural byway winding through rural countryside, past rambling stone walls, scattered old homes, and the barns and crop fields of working farms. It traces the rural border of New Hampshire and Maine, rolling up and down through woods and occasionally hugging the shore of one of the many lakes in this isolated region.

Wakefield Corners is a picture-perfect cluster of more than two-dozen 18th- and 19th-century homes, including the Wakefield Inn, a handsome 1804 Federal building, and the Museum of Childhood, a personal collection of more than five thousand dolls, toys, and stuffed animals. Down the road, Pine River Pond, Balch Pond, Sand

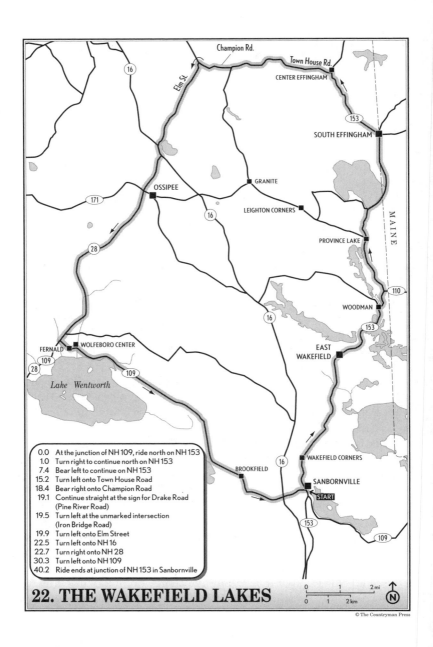

Champion Rd.

Town House Rd.

16

Elm St.

CENTER EFFINGHAM

153

SOUTH EFFINGHAM

171

GRANITE

OSSIPEE

16

LEIGHTON CORNERS

28

PROVINCE LAKE

M A I N E

110

16

WOODMAN

153

FERNALD

WOLFEBORO CENTER

EAST
WAKEFIELD

109
28

109

Lake Wentworth

0.0 At the junction of NH 109, ride north on NH 153
1.0 Turn right to continue north on NH 153
7.4 Bear left to continue on NH 153
15.2 Turn left onto Town House Road
18.4 Bear right onto Champion Road
19.1 Continue straight at the sign for Drake Road
       (Pine River Road)
19.5 Turn left at the unmarked intersection
       (Iron Bridge Road)
19.9 Turn left onto Elm Street
22.5 Turn left onto NH 16
22.7 Turn right onto NH 28
30.3 Turn left onto NH 109
40.2 Ride ends at junction of NH 153 in Sanbornville

BROOKFIELD

16

WAKEFIELD CORNERS

SANBORNVILLE

START

153

109

0   1   2 mi
0   1   2 km

22. THE WAKEFIELD LAKES

N

© The Countryman Press

Pond, Belleau Lake, and Province Lake are all strung along a 4-mile stretch. Center Effingham is a ghost of a village, with a couple of ornate white clapboard buildings perched on a quiet hillside.

The final leg of the tour passes the shoreline of Lake Wentworth and the Governor Wentworth Historic Site, the location of the 18th-century summer estate of New Hampshire's last royal governor. It was Wentworth who laid out a road that connected Portsmouth to Dartmouth College in Hanover via Lake Winnipesaukee. This key east-west route across the state is known alternately as College Road and Governors Road.

DIRECTIONS FOR THE RIDE

The ride begins in the center of Sanbornville. Parking is available across the street from the brick town offices and library building. There are several markets and convenience stores along the way.

0.0 At the junction of NH 109, ride north on NH 153.
Immediately begin a winding half-mile climb.

1.0 In Wakefield Corners, turn right to continue north on NH 153.

2.3 Use caution crossing the railroad tracks.

6.1 Ride past a trio of ponds—Pine River Pond, Balch Pond, and Sand Pond.

7.0 Pass through the hamlet of Woodman, at the southern tip of Belleau Lake.

7.4 At the junction of NH 110 and 153, bear left to continue on NH 153 (NH 110 heads east to Newfield, Maine).
The corner market at this crossroads on the state line sells two dozen flavors of soft-serve ice cream.

9.7 Use caution on the steep descent to the shore of Belleau Lake.
The White Mountains provide a dramatic backdrop on the western horizon.

15.2 Turn left onto Town House Road.
Ride toward the ornate white clapboard buildings, now housing Effington's town offices and library. Beyond the village, the road passes through a mix of meadow and forest.

The rural Maine border is a pleasing mix of lakes and forest.

18.4 At the unmarked Y-intersection, bear right on Champion Road.
Use caution on the short, steep downhill.

19.1 At the stop sign, continue straight at the sign for Drake Road (Pine River Road).

19.5 Turn left onto Iron Bridge Road at the unmarked intersection.

19.9 At the next Y-intersection, turn left onto Elm Street.

20.7 Cross the Ossipee town line.

22.2 Ride past Duncan Lake.
The road winds around the lakeshore past small cottages.

22.5 At the stop sign, turn left onto NH 16.
The Route 16 Dairy Bar is on this corner.

22.7 Just past the Dairy Bar, turn right onto NH 28, heading toward Wolfeboro.

30.3 In Wolfeboro Center, turn left onto NH 109.

40.2 The ride ends at the junction of NH 153 in Sanbornville.

Bicycle Shops

Mountain Sports, NH 3 and 106, Meredith; 603-279-5540

Ski Works, NH 16, West Ossipee; 603-539-2246

Wolfeboro Sports Outlet, 36 Glendon Street, Wolfeboro; 603-569-5777

Nordic Skier Sports, 47 North Main Street, Wolfeboro; 603-569-3151

THE
WHITE
MOUNTAINS

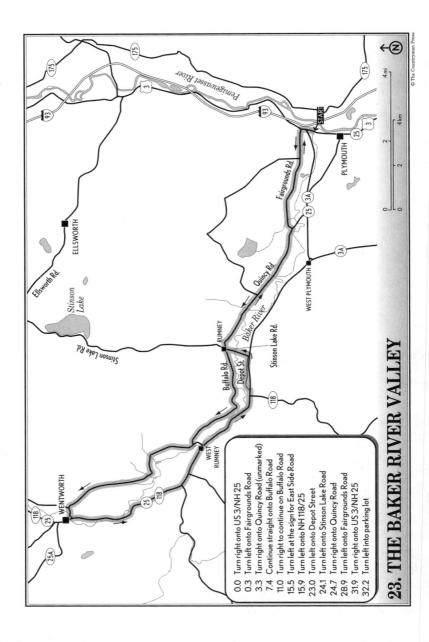

0.0	Turn right onto US 3/NH 25
0.3	Turn left onto Fairgrounds Road
3.3	Turn right onto Quincy Road (unmarked)
7.4	Continue straight onto Buffalo Road
11.0	Turn right to continue on Buffalo Road
15.5	Turn left at the sign for East Side Road
15.9	Turn left onto NH 118/25
23.0	Turn left onto Depot Street
24.1	Turn left onto Stinson Lake Road
24.7	Turn right onto Quincy Road
28.9	Turn left onto Fairgrounds Road
31.9	Turn right onto US 3/NH 25
32.2	Turn left into parking lot

23. THE BAKER RIVER VALLEY

© The Countryman Press

The Baker River Valley

- **DISTANCE:** 32.2 miles (30 miles if you complete the tour via Stinson Lake)
- **TERRAIN:** Flat and rolling; a 1-mile stretch of dirt surface on Buffalo Road
- **DIFFICULTY:** Moderate/Strenuous, via Stinson Lake
- **RECOMMENDED BICYCLE:** Touring/road bike; mountain bike or hybrid for the Stinson Lake route

There is a network of lightly traveled country lanes on the outskirts of Plymouth that cuts through the gentle terrain of the Baker River valley, a landscape of farms and open space on the extreme southern fringe of the White Mountain National Forest. The Baker River begins at Mount Moosilauke, the westernmost of the White Mountains, and eventually converges with the Pemigewasset River in Plymouth.

Farm stands along the way sell locally grown produce and maple syrup. Sometimes the road climbs into the woods, but most often it rolls gently along, following the slow course of the river.

Rumney is another of New Hampshire's classic white clapboard New England villages. Its location well off the beaten path lends an air of authenticity that's lost on some heavily visited historic sites. In town is the Mary Baker Eddy House, where the founder of the Christian Science Church lived in the 1860s. Rumney is a peaceful cluster of historic buildings surrounded by neat picket fences. The small tree-lined green has many benches that seem to beckon

The Baker River valley sits on the western edge of the vast White Mountain National Forest.

passersby to stop awhile and experience the peace and solitude.

Buffalo Road is a remote byway that you'll likely have to yourself, although you may see rock climbers preparing to tackle the steep cliffs north of the road. An occasional house or open meadow breaks up the thick woods on the way to Wentworth, a tranquil community centered on a grassy common set above the Baker River.

An optional route to isolated Stinson Lake includes a challenging climb and descent on a dirt road into the rugged hills just to the north of Rumney. If you plan to take this side trip, a mountain bike or hybrid is recommended, since there is a 3-mile dirt section.

Plymouth is best known as the home of Plymouth State College, and has a decent selection of shops and restaurants for a town with four thousand students. The New Hampshire Music Festival brings chamber and orchestra music here every summer.

DIRECTIONS FOR THE RIDE

The ride begins in the parking area in front of the Plymouth Chamber of Commerce and Rhino Bike Works in Plymouth. The lot is just before the green steel bridge leading into Plymouth on US 3/NH 25.

0.0 From the parking area, turn right onto US 3/NH 25.
Use caution on this main road that crosses over I-93.

0.3 Turn left onto Fairgrounds Road, just past the junction of NH 3A and NH 25.
A quiet neighborhood of modest homes soon gives way to wide-open farmland backed by peaks on this gently rolling country road along the Baker River.

3.3 At the stop sign, turn right onto Quincy Road (unmarked; the intersection is at the edge of a long field).
For a quick detour, take a left to the Smith Millennium Covered Bridge. You'll see it from here.

5.3 Ride past the entrance to the Quincy Bog Natural Area.
This 40-acre peat bog has walking trails, a viewing platform, and a nature center.

7.4 At the grassy common in the village of Rumney, continue straight onto Buffalo Road.
Side trip: To complete this tour via Stinson Lake, turn right at the common onto Stinson Lake Road, where you'll begin a leg-burning 5-mile climb. If you accept

the challenge, you will be treated to stunning views of the White Mountains while you enjoy one of the most remote places in the area. Past the lake, make a long, steep descent on Ellsworth Road to US 3, which will take you south to Plymouth.

11.0 At the T-intersection, turn right to continue on Buffalo Road.
This junction is unmarked, so just look for the small cemetery surrounded by a white picket fence on the corner.

15.5 At the stop sign, turn left at the sign for East Side Road.

15.8 Cross the steel bridge to take a side trip to the Colonial village of Wentworth.
At the time of this writing, the bridge was closed for repairs; you can reach Wentworth on NH 25. Vintage homes, a white clapboard church and library, a tiny post office, and an even tinier historical museum flank the long, narrow green of this village, incorporated in 1766.

15.9 At the stop sign, turn left onto NH 118/25.
This busy road has a wide shoulder to ride on, plus two convenience stores for food and supplies.

23.0 At the Montessori school, turn left onto Depot Street.

24.1 At the stop sign, turn left onto Stinson Lake Road.

24.7 In the center of Rumney, turn right at the village green onto Quincy Road.
From here, you will retrace the route back to Plymouth.

28.9 Turn left onto Fairgrounds Road.

31.9 At the stop sign, turn right onto US 3/NH 25 south.

32.2 Turn left into the parking lot to end the ride.

Bicycle Shops

Rhino Bike Works, 95 South Main Street, Plymouth; 603-536-3919

Ski Fanatics, NH 49, Campton; 603-726-4327

Joe Jones Ski and Sports, NH 49, Campton; 603-726-3000

24

Sugar Hill

- **DISTANCE:** 23.3 miles
- **TERRAIN:** Rolling hills with two very steep climbs
- **DIFFICULTY:** Strenuous
- **RECOMMENDED BICYCLE:** Touring/road bike

To millions of visitors, the Franconia area is synonymous with the craggy profile of the Old Man of the Mountain, a protruding rock 1,200 feet up Cannon Mountain that resembled the side of an old man's face. It was a beloved icon for locals and tourists ever since it was first spotted by pioneers in 1805 high above Profile Lake. On May 3, 2003, the 40-foot-tall stone profile fell. The 200-million-year-old granite boulders were held in place for almost a century with the help of steel cables, until they simply slid loose, and the Old Man was reduced to a pile of rubble. Just like that, New Hampshire lost its most recognizable feature, the official state symbol since 1945, which adorned license plates, the state quarter, road signs, and tourist brochures.

Thankfully, Franconia still has much to offer, including the Flume Gorge, Franconia Notch State Park, Cannon Mountain's aerial tramway, and museums dedicated to Robert Frost, the iron ore industry, and the history of New England skiing. Its peaceful back roads appeal to cyclists looking to escape the bustle of this popular tourist destination. This hilly but beautiful ride explores the high wooded country between the historic villages of Franconia and Sugar Hill.

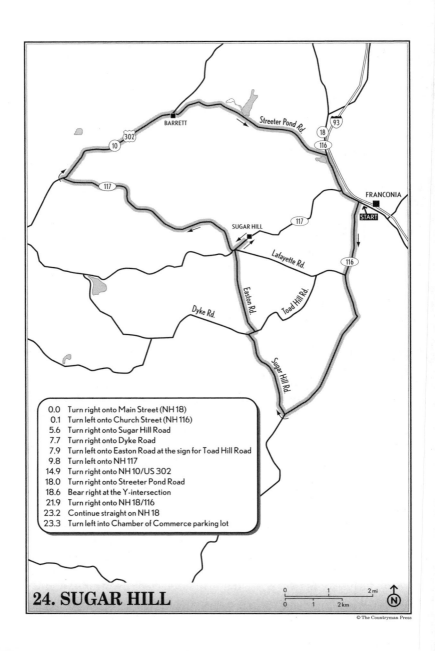

0.0 Turn right onto Main Street (NH 18)
0.1 Turn left onto Church Street (NH 116)
5.6 Turn right onto Sugar Hill Road
7.7 Turn right onto Dyke Road
7.9 Turn left onto Easton Road at the sign for Toad Hill Road
9.8 Turn left onto NH 117
14.9 Turn right onto NH 10/US 302
18.0 Turn right onto Streeter Pond Road
18.6 Bear right at the Y-intersection
21.9 Turn right onto NH 18/116
23.2 Continue straight on NH 18
23.3 Turn left into Chamber of Commerce parking lot

24. SUGAR HILL

0   1   2 mi
0   1   2 km

N

© The Countryman Press

Franconia is a friendly town in the shadow of the Presidentials that attracts a wide range of visitors, from backcountry hikers and downhill skiers to the tourists who've been lured by the awe-inspiring scenery for centuries. Its shops, eateries, museums, and natural attractions make this a good place to explore after the ride.

Sugar Hill is set back into the hills, on a ridge high above the Ammonoosuc Valley. It's a handsome, gleaming-white village surrounded by open hilltop acres that have been farmed since the 18th century. In the 1920s, this was the site of the first ski school in the country. Sugar Hill is known for its collection of vintage buildings, including inns, churches, a historical museum, and a general store. Perhaps more enticing are the striking views of the Presidential and Franconia Ranges, especially from Sunset Hill. The panorama is memorable at any time but extraordinarily beautiful during foliage season, when the ridges are blazing with color.

DIRECTIONS FOR THE RIDE

The ride begins in Franconia at the Franconia–Sugar Hill–Easton Chamber of Commerce on Main Street (NH 18). You can pick up supplies in town before the ride.

0.0 Turn right out of the chamber of commerce parking lot onto Main Street (NH 18), heading north toward Franconia village.

0.1 At the blinking traffic light, turn left onto Church Street (NH 116). *Cross the Gale River, then pass through a neighborhood of historic homes that gives way to rural countryside.*

1.0 Pass the entrance road to the Robert Frost Museum (Bickford Hill Road). *Relics from Frost's career as New England's favorite poet fill the meticulously restored 1859 farmhouse, which now hosts poetry readings, writing workshops, and a summertime poet-in-residence program.*

2.1 Past the Franconia Inn and the Franconia Village Cross-Country Ski Center, the road starts to roll up toward Easton.

5.6 Turn right onto Sugar Hill Road. *This narrow back road climbs through the woods for 2 miles in one of the route's*

A scenic back road in the hills above Franconia

most arduous ascents. Towering pines give way to the occasional hilltop meadow along the way.

7.7 At the stop sign, turn right onto Dyke Road, following the sign for Sugar Hill.
The vintage stone house on the corner is reminiscent of what this rural hill community was like centuries ago.

7.9 At the bottom of the hill, turn left onto Easton Road at the sign for Toad Hill Road.
There's still some climbing left to get to Sugar Hill, but it's tempered with flat sections and descents.

9.8 At the stop sign, turn left and begin the descent to Lisbon on NH 117 (a half mile to the right is the village of Sugar Hill).

A side trip to this picturesque hilltop is a must. Check out the prim clapboard buildings, vintage farms, charming inns, and antiques shops. Pick up some local cheese and maple syrup at Harman's Country Store. Find Sunset Hill Road for one of the best panoramas around.

14.9 At the stop sign, turn right onto NH 10/US 302.
Enjoy the expansive views as you ride through the rural valley that follows the curves of the wide Ammonoosuc River.

18.0 Turn right onto Streeter Pond Road.
Cross the bridge and head up into the hills for the second and final challenge of the route, a steep 1.5-mile climb.

18.6 At the Y-intersection, bear right.

19.7 Ride along the southern tip of Streeter Pond.
From here, you'll begin the descent that will bring you to the farming valley along the Gale River on the outskirts of Franconia.

21.9 At the yield sign, turn right onto NH 18/116, heading south toward Franconia.
Use caution when riding through the small, busy village.

23.2 At the blinking traffic light, continue straight on NH 18.

23.3 Turn left into the chamber of commerce parking lot to end the ride.

Bicycle Shops

Littleton Bike Shop, 87 Main Street (US 302), Littleton; 603-444-3437; www .littletonbike.com

White Mountain Cyclist, 143 Main Street (NH 112), Lincoln; 603-745-8852

Ski and Bike Warehouse, 112 Main Street (NH 112), Lincoln; 603-745-3164

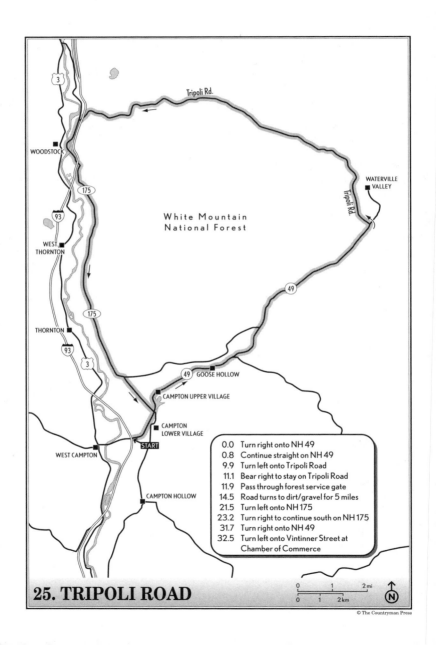

Tripoli Rd.

3

WOODSTOCK

175

93

WEST THORNTON

THORNTON

93

3

175

White Mountain
National Forest

WATERVILLE VALLEY

Tripoli Rd.

49

49 GOOSE HOLLOW

CAMPTON UPPER VILLAGE

CAMPTON
LOWER VILLAGE

WEST CAMPTON START

CAMPTON HOLLOW

0.0	Turn right onto NH 49
0.8	Continue straight on NH 49
9.9	Turn left onto Tripoli Road
11.1	Bear right to stay on Tripoli Road
11.9	Pass through forest service gate
14.5	Road turns to dirt/gravel for 5 miles
21.5	Turn left onto NH 175
23.2	Turn right to continue south on NH 175
31.7	Turn right onto NH 49
32.5	Turn left onto Vintinner Street at Chamber of Commerce

25. TRIPOLI ROAD

0   1   2 mi
0   1   2 km

N

© The Countryman Press

Tripoli Road

- **DISTANCE:** 32.5
- **TERRAIN:** Rolling and hilly; a 5-mile section of hard-packed dirt road
- **DIFFICULTY:** Strenuous
- **RECOMMENDED BICYCLE:** Mountain bike/hybrid

Waterville Valley is an isolated ravine on the southwestern edge of the White Mountains that is synonymous with New Hampshire skiing. The Mad River cuts a long, deep swath into this ragged mountain chain of many 4,000-footers, including Mount Tecumseh and Mount Osceola. This tour climbs into the valley on a scenic national forest highway and returns on the wildly remote Tripoli Road, a rural forest road that snakes through the mountains between the Sandwich Range and the Pemigewasset Wilderness Areas, one of the largest tracts of undisturbed backcountry in the East.

Visitors discovered Waterville Valley in the 1800s. For them, it was a peaceful mountain retreat, with only one hotel surrounded by pristine wilderness. It didn't become a skiing destination until the 1930s, when a few trails were cut on Mount Tecumseh and Snow's Mountain. The real boom came in the 1960s, when former Olympic skier Tom Corcoran opened a ski resort modeled after Aspen, Vail, and others out West. Today it's a thriving year-round holiday destination, especially popular with families.

The rugged Tripoli Road harks back to what mountain travel in

the Whites was like centuries ago. The roughly 10-mile road—
partly paved, otherwise dirt—is a lofty mountain byway and a
popular automobile foliage loop in autumn. It starts high in
Waterville Valley, passes between Mount Tecumseh and Mount
Osceola, reaches its high point of 2,300 feet in the lofty Thornton
Gap, and then drops far below to the Pemigewasset River and
I-93 in Woodstock.

Riding into the valley, the Whites spread out before you, but it's
only a small corner of this vast 768,000-acre forest, created by the
Weeks Act in 1911. The 19th century marked the birth of New
Hampshire's logging industry, when large stands of thick virgin
forest were clear-cut from mountainsides, leaving the land prone
to erosion, forest fires, and flooding. Concerned residents and long-
time visitors formed an environmental group that pushed local
politician John Weeks to promote a bill granting the mountains
protective status. As a result, the White Mountain National Forest
became the first national forest in the country, and remains the
largest in the Northeast. The forest service still harvests timber
on a much smaller scale, but not in any of the four designated
leave-no-trace wilderness areas.

The ride begins in Campton, a quiet village with a few bed &
breakfasts and a handful of eateries. There is a general store in
town where you can pick up supplies and another in Waterville
Valley, at the beginning of Tripoli Road.

On Tripoli Road, use caution when riding past the trailheads,
where hikers are often crossing the road. Particularly busy are
the trailheads for the Mount Osceola Trail and the Mount
Tecumseh Trail; the latter is a popular hike since it's one of the
easiest 4,000-footers in the Whites to summit. Remember that
often people on foot don't even hear a bike until it's right behind
them. As a courtesy, make them aware of your presence and slow
your pace as you pass.

DIRECTIONS FOR THE RIDE
The tour begins at the Waterville Valley Regional Chamber of Commerce on
NH 49, at Exit 28 off I-93. There's a market in Campton and a convenience
store at the beginning of Tripoli Road about 10 miles into the ride.

Storm clouds scuttling across the high peaks of the White Mountains

0.0 From the parking area on Vintinner Street, turn right onto NH 49.
Begin the steady climb along the Mad River to the village of Campton.

0.8 At the traffic light continue straight on NH 49, riding along the Campton Pond.
Soon you'll enter the White Mountain National Forest. The road follows the Mad River on a long, moderate climb that cuts through the mountains into Waterville Valley.

9.9 Turn left onto Tripoli Road at the sign for Waterville Valley Ski Area.

11.1 At the Y-intersection, bear right to stay on Tripoli Road.
It seems like this narrow forest road is leading you deep into the mountains. You'll pass several trailheads and picnic areas.

11.9 Pass through the forest service gate.
The road surface is paved but rough and potholed in places, so use appropriate caution.

14.5 The road surface turns to hard-packed dirt and gravel here for about 5 miles.
Use caution on this section and watch for potholes and rough areas. From here, you'll begin the long descent—very steep in places—that will take you out of the national forest and toward Thornton.

21.5 At the stop sign near I-93, turn left onto NH 175, heading south to Campton.
Scattered homes are a sign that you're heading back to civilization.

23.2 Turn right at the sign for Gore Road to continue south on NH 175.
These woods in Thornton are heavily developed with residential subdivisions and condominiums; thankfully, entrance signs are usually all you'll see from the road.

31.7 At the traffic light in Campton, turn right onto NH 49.
The blue Campton Cupboard General Store is in the center of the village.

32.5 Turn left onto Vintinner Street at the chamber of commerce to end the ride.

Bicycle Shops

Rhino Bike Works, 95 South Main Street, Plymouth; 603-536-3919

Ski Fanatics, NH 49, Campton; 603-726-4327

Joe Jones Ski and Sports, NH 49, Campton; 603-726-3000

26

The Kancamagus Highway via Bear Notch

- **DISTANCE:** 37.4 miles
- **TERRAIN:** Flat valley terrain, with a steep 5-mile climb to Bear Notch
- **DIFFICULTY:** Strenuous/Two optional easy routes
- **RECOMMENDED BICYCLE:** Touring/road bike

The frenetic strip of motels, family resorts, restaurants, and factory outlets in North Conway are quite close to this tour, but if you drive into town from the west, you'd never know it. Here you'll find a rare mix of high peaks and working farmland. Cornfields, barns, silos, and pastures create a pastoral foreground for the majesty of the surrounding White Mountain National Forest. Toss in a dramatic mountain pass, three covered bridges, and a spin on one of the most famous scenic byways in the country, and you have a phenomenal ride—and a relatively flat and easy one—through New England's highest mountain range.

The tour begins on West Side Road, beloved by local cyclists who want to experience the splendor of the White Mountains without the usual climbing. Instead, wide fields of corn and hay stretch through a rural farming valley on the banks of the Saco River and north to the ski town of Bartlett. You'll climb up to Bear Notch, a high mountain pass that serves as a shortcut to the Kancamagus National Scenic Byway. Known around here as the "Kanc," this 34.5-mile scenic road hugs the curves of the Swift River and climbs nearly 3,000 feet as it crosses east to west through the heart of the

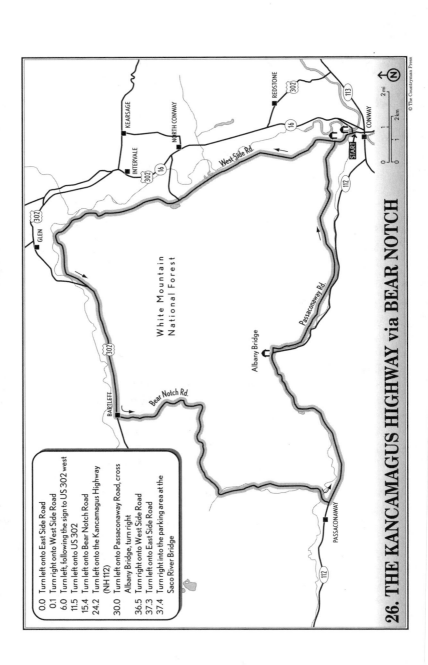

0.0   Turn left onto East Side Road
0.1   Turn right onto West Side Road
6.0   Turn left, following the sign to US 302 west
11.5 Turn left onto US 302
15.4 Turn left onto Bear Notch Road
24.2 Turn left onto the Kancamagus Highway
      (NH 112)
30.0 Turn left onto Passaconaway Road, cross
      Albany Bridge, turn right
36.5 Turn right onto West Side Road
37.3 Turn left onto East Side Road
37.4 Turn right into the parking area at the
      Saco River Bridge

26. THE KANCAMAGUS HIGHWAY via BEAR NOTCH

White Mountain
National Forest

Bear Notch Rd.

Albany Bridge

Passaconaway Rd.

West Side Rd.

BARTLETT

GLEN

INTERVALE

KEARSAGE

NORTH CONWAY

REDSTONE

CONWAY

START

PASSACONAWAY

302

302

302

16

16

112

112

113

N

2 mi

2 km

0   1   2 mi
0   1   2 km

© The Countryman Press

Whites. Finally, you'll cross a historic covered bridge to Passaconaway Road, named for the logging and farming settlement that once thrived here, then return to Conway.

This tour offers plenty of hard-to-resist detours. The ride is barely underway before you'll see a pair of historic covered bridges, the 1890 Saco River Bridge in quiet Conway Village and the 1869 Swift River Bridge just up the road. The latter is open to foot traffic only and has a few picnic tables that make for a good post-ride stop.

Farther along West Side Road are Echo Lake State Park, a picturesque lake at the base of White Horse Ledge; Diana's Baths, a series of potholes carved by water and time at the base of a cascade in Lucy Brook; and Cathedral Ledge, a high promontory affording spectacular views into the valley below. North Conway is a mecca for rock climbing, as Cathedral and Whitehorse Cliffs are two of the top granite crags in the country. The northern section of Bear Notch Road has a few overlooks that offer stunning views of the surrounding peaks and Crawford Notch. Finally, along the Kancamagus you'll pass the Rocky Gorge Scenic Area and a couple of picnic areas on Passaconaway Road.

There are two options for shorter, easier rides in this area. One is an 11.5-mile ride north on West Side Road, simply returning the way you came. The other choice is to take Passaconaway Road west to the Albany Bridge, then return to Conway on the Kancamagus Highway for a loop of about 15 miles.

DIRECTIONS FOR THE RIDE

The ride begins in Conway at the Davis Park Recreation Area on East Side Road at the 1890 Saco River Covered Bridge.

0.0 Turn left out of the parking lot and cross the Saco River on the covered bridge.

0.1 At the stop sign, turn right onto West Side Road.
This scenic back road is a cyclist's delight. When not passing effortlessly through flat farmland, it just rolls along gently. Farms along the way offer everything from strawberries and corn to pumpkins and maple syrup, and herds of horses and cows graze peacefully in fields.

0.2 Pass by the Swift River Covered Bridge.
The historic bridge is open to pedestrians only.

5.6 Pass the entrance to Echo Lake State Park.

6.0 Turn left at the stop sign, following the sign to US 302 west and Bartlett.
Along the way you'll pass entrances to Cathedral Ledge and Diana's Baths. If you don't stop during the ride, you may want to return to them later.

11.5 At the stop sign, turn left onto US 302, heading west toward Bartlett.
Red Jersey Cyclery is just ahead, stop in for supplies or to get advice on other local rides. A little farther on, the slopes of the Attitash Bear Peak ski resort come into view.

15.0 Ride into the village of Bartlett.
The Bear Notch Deli & Market is a good stop for food and supplies before climbing into the mountains.

The Albany Covered Bridge spans the Swift River west of Conway.

15.4 At the blinking traffic light, turn left onto Bear Notch Road.
This is where the climbing begins. At the gate, which closes this mountain pass in the winter, you'll enter the White Mountain National Forest. Stop at the handful of overlooks to rest and enjoy the panoramic views of the surrounding mountains.

20.3 Begin the descent down the other side of Bear Notch.
Use caution on the winding downhill road.

24.2 At the stop sign, turn left onto the Kancamagus Highway (NH 112), heading east toward Conway.
Enjoy the gradual downhill along the Swift River, with peaks and sheer cliffs above the road.

30.0 Turn left onto Passaconaway Road and ride over the Albany Bridge, turning right at the other end.
This narrow, tree-lined side road on the other side of the Swift River offers the beauty of the Kancamagus without the traffic. The parking lot for the Boulder Loop Trail has an access to the river for great views of the 1858 covered bridge. If you don't stop here, there are plenty of spots along the way to enjoy the views.

36.5 At the stop sign, turn right onto West Side Road.

37.3 At the green, turn left onto East Side Road.

37.4 Turn right into the parking area at the Saco River Bridge to end the ride.

Bicycle Shops

Red Jersey Cyclery, US 302, Bartlett; 603-374-2700; www.redjerseycyclery.com

The Bike Shop, Mountain Valley Mall Boulevard, North Conway; 603-356-6089

Joe Jones Ski and Sports, 2709 Main Street (NH 16), North Conway; 603-356-9411

Sports Outlet, Main Street (NH 16), North Conway; 603-356-3133

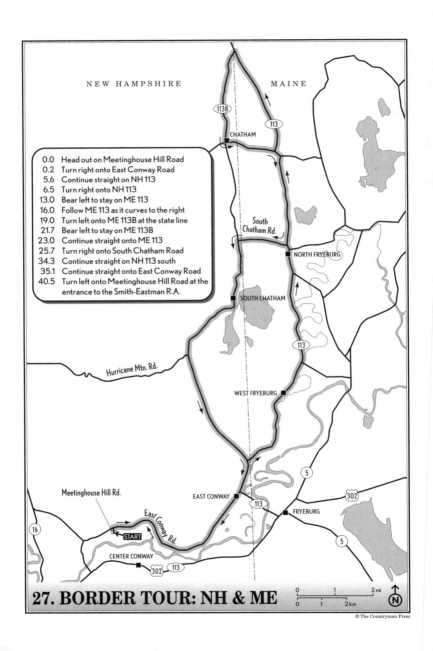

NEW HAMPSHIRE   MAINE

113B

CHATHAM

113

0.0	Head out on Meetinghouse Hill Road
0.2	Turn right onto East Conway Road
5.6	Continue straight on NH 113
6.5	Turn right onto NH 113
13.0	Bear left to stay on ME 113
16.0	Follow ME 113 as it curves to the right
19.0	Turn left onto ME 113B at the state line
21.7	Bear left to stay on ME 113B
23.0	Continue straight onto ME 113
25.7	Turn right onto South Chatham Road
34.3	Continue straight on NH 113 south
35.1	Continue straight onto East Conway Road
40.5	Turn left onto Meetinghouse Hill Road at the entrance to the Smith-Eastman R.A.

South Chatham Rd.

NORTH FRYEBURG

SOUTH CHATHAM

113

Hurricane Mtn. Rd.

WEST FRYEBURG

5

302

Meetinghouse Hill Rd.

EAST CONWAY

113

FRYEBURG

16

East Conway Rd.

START

5

CENTER CONWAY

302   113

27. BORDER TOUR: NH & ME

0		1		2 mi
0	1		2 km	

N

Border Tour: New Hampshire and Maine

- **DISTANCE:** 40.5 miles
- **TERRAIN:** Flat roads and rolling hills
- **DIFFICULTY:** Moderate to strenuous
- **RECOMMENDED BICYCLE:** Touring/road bike

This route skirts the remote border of New Hampshire and Maine, a pastoral landscape of wide-open farmland, dense forest, and the foothills of the White Mountains. North Fryeburg, Maine, is one of the most rural villages in this book, little more than a quiet intersection fronted by rambling old clapboard homes.

This is the kind of bucolic countryside where the roads are wonderfully empty, and most homes are accompanied by at least one barn. Some farms are thriving, with a farmhouse, barns, and fenced pastures standing neat and proud. Others have clearly seen better times, or have been abandoned altogether. Along the way, stores sell snowmobiles, woodstoves, and guns; produce stands offer potatoes, honey, eggs, and vegetables.

Although mountain ranges are omnipresent, remember that you're riding on the *edge* of the Whites, so even the most strenuous climbs are tame considering your rugged surroundings. In Maine, the lofty peaks of the Caribou Speckled Mountain Wilderness to the north create a dramatic backdrop; you'll turn back toward New Hampshire just before reaching them.

The ride begins at the Smith-Eastman Recreation Area, a popular local spot on the Saco River east of Conway. There is a canoe launching area as well as a jogging and biking path along the river. Don't be dismayed by the traffic and activity on well-traveled NH 113; the tour slips off the beaten path as you ride into Maine.

DIRECTIONS FOR THE RIDE

The ride begins in East Conway. Park at the Smith-Eastman Recreation Area on Meetinghouse Hill Road, off East Conway Road between the police department and the Saco River. There are no bike shops along the way, so be sure to carry adequate supplies.

0.0 Head out of the parking lot on Meetinghouse Hill Road.

0.2 At the stop sign, turn right onto East Conway Road.
Homes and small businesses line the road, less frequently as you head out of town. The scenery changes to woods, old barns, grazing sheep, and flat farmland the closer you get to the Maine border.

5.6 Continue straight on NH 113.

6.5 Turn right onto NH 113 just past the old firehouse, crossing into West Fryeburg, Maine.

12.4 Pass through North Fryeburg.
This quiet, faded hamlet is marked by the white clapboard 1838 Universalist Chapel at the edge of a cornfield. The Harbor Restaurant and General Store may seem like a strange name for a business in this rural farming community, but it refers to the town of Fryeburg Harbor (near Maine's Kezar Lake) just to the east.

13.0 At the intersection of Harbor Road, bear left to stay on ME 113, following the signs to North Chatham and Stow.

16.0 At the Stow Corner Store, follow ME 113 as it curves to the right.
The market is a modest yellow clapboard building that serves the residents scattered throughout these rural hills. The pizza, ice cream, baked goods, and sandwiches make this a worthwhile stop, either now or when the ride circles back later on.

19.0 Turn left onto ME 113B at the state line; there is a sign here for Main Road.
You can buy fresh eggs, honey, and pumpkins from farmhouses along this road.

The Conway area is popular with cyclists.

21.7 Bear left at the white Chatham Congregational Church and tiny library to stay on ME 113B.

23.0 At the stop sign, continue straight onto ME 113, heading south past the Stow Country Store.

25.7 Turn right onto South Chatham Road.
Ride straight toward the New Hampshire state line and the rugged peaks of the White Mountains in the distance.

26.9 Cross into Chatham, New Hampshire (unmarked).
Although this is basically one long stretch of unmarked road with no intersections, the name changes to Robbins Ridge Road where the road turns south to follow the state line. When you cross into Conway, the name changes again to Green Hill Road, but it's also unmarked.

34.3 Continue straight on NH 113 south.

35.1 At the junction of NH 113, continue straight onto East Conway Road.

40.5 Turn left onto Meetinghouse Hill Road at the entrance to the Smith-Eastman Recreation Area to end the ride.

Bicycle Shops

The Bike Shop, Mountain Valley Mall Boulevard, North Conway; 603-356-6089

Joe Jones Ski and Sports, 2709 Main Street (NH 16), North Conway; 603-356-9411

Sports Outlet, Main Street (NH 16), North Conway; 603-356-3133

THE GREAT
NORTH WOODS

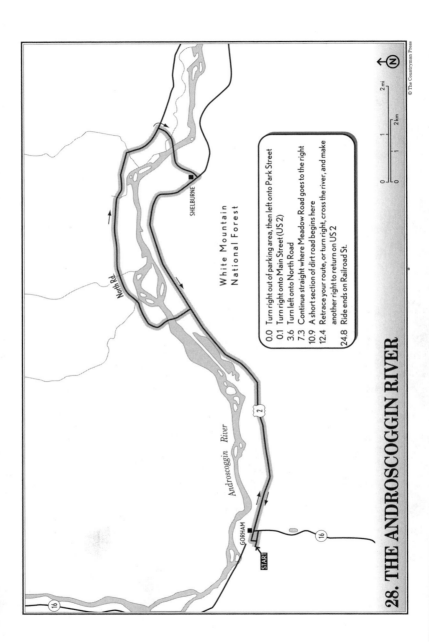

28. THE ANDROSCOGGIN RIVER

0.0 Turn right out of parking area, then left onto Park Street
0.1 Turn right onto Main Street (US 2)
3.6 Turn left onto North Road
7.3 Continue straight where Meadow Road goes to the right
10.9 A short section of dirt road begins here
12.4 Retrace your route, or turn right, cross the river, and make another right to return on US 2
24.8 Ride ends on Railroad St.

White Mountain
National Forest

SHELBURNE

North Rd.

Androscoggin   River

GORHAM

START

© The Countryman Press

28

The Androscoggin River

- **DISTANCE:** 24.8 miles
- **TERRAIN:** Rolling hills mixed with flat sections
- **DIFFICULTY:** Easy to moderate
- **RECOMMENDED BICYCLE:** Touring/road bike

The Androscoggin River slices along New Hampshire's remote northeastern border, through brick mill towns on the way to its confluence with the Kenebec River in Maine. The relative lack of tourists on these quiet valley roads makes this ride through Gorham and Shelburne, New Hampshire blissfully peaceful.

Old-time back roads twist along the slow-flowing Androscoggin, known around here as the "Andy," a mighty waterway that local environmentalists helped transform from a polluted embarrassment to a pristine river teeming with wildlife. At one time, industrial waste from upriver pulp and paper mills threatened the river's future. Thanks to a massive cleanup effort by local environmentalists in the last few decades, the Androscoggin has made a stunning comeback. Today it's a popular playground for fishermen and canoeists. In Gorham, the river changes its southerly flow and heads east toward Maine.

The river's source is north in Errol at Lake Umbagog, a sprawling 15,000-acre national wildlife refuge that, like the river, is shared by both states. In the background are the massive hulks of the White Mountain National Forest's Presidential Range.

Lofty peaks are a familiar backdrop in New Hampshire's North Country.

Gorham's industrial roots are inextricably linked to this mighty river, which fueled the lumber mills here in the 19th century. Indeed, it was the byproducts of this local industry that played a large part in the river's past decline. The town also boomed in this era because it was a stop along the Atlantic and St. Lawrence Railroad, which hauled tourists from Maine into the White Mountains. On Railroad Street, where the tour begins, stands the Railroad Station Museum, home to the Gorham Historical Society and displays on the town's logging and railroad history.

Gorham remains a popular hub with visitors, many of whom use it as a base to explore the White Mountains to the south or as a stop off before heading to the Great North Woods for fishing, hunting, canoeing, even moose watching. Tour operators in Gorham shuttle visitors through the thick forests north of town to see the massive animals, the largest wild creatures in New Hampshire.

The route follows the Androscoggin toward Maine on US 2. This is the North Country's main east-west road, so expect traffic, often in the form of large commercial trucks, many piled high with freshly hewn timber. After a few miles, the ride leaves this road, crosses the river, and heads east on a much quieter route.

You'll pass an occasional homestead or farm scattered along rural North Road. On US 2 you'll pass the 19th-century clapboard Mount Washington Bed & Breakfast and the pristine birch grove that stands as a war memorial to local soldiers who gave their lives for their country.

This ride can be completed one of two ways. The most scenic and enjoyable route is to go out and back on the rural road north of the river. To make a loop, you can return to Gorham on scenic-yet-busy US 2.

DIRECTIONS FOR THE RIDE

The tour begins in the center of Gorham on Main Street (US 2). Start from the public parking area on Railroad Street, just behind Main Street near the town common. There are markets in town for supplies.

0.0 Turn right out of the parking area, then left onto Park Street, passing between the Gorham Police Department and the baseball field on the town common.

0.1 At the stop sign, turn right onto Main Street (US 2).
Once you leave downtown behind, dramatic mountain views will open up.

2.3 Ride past the memorial birch forest.

3.6 Turn left onto North Road.
This is the best part of the ride, what backroad cycling is all about. After crossing the Androscoggin, this idyllic road winds above and along the river, past forests, scattered old homes, farms, meadows, grazing sheep and horses—a landscape that seems untouched by the 21st century.

7.3 At the Y-intersection, continue straight where Meadow Road goes to the right.

10.9 A short section of dirt road begins here; use caution.

12.4 At the stop sign, you have a choice to make: retrace your steps along the rural back road, or turn right, cross the river, and make another right to return to Gorham on US 2.

24.8 The ride ends on Railroad Street in downtown Gorham.

Bicycle Shops

Moriah Sports, 101 Main Street (US 2), Gorham; 603-466-5050; www.moriahsports.com

29

Berlin to Milan

- **DISTANCE:** 27.9 miles
- **TERRAIN:** Rolling and steep hills
- **DIFFICULTY:** Sstrenuous
- **RECOMMENDED BICYCLE:** Touring/road bike

The mountainous Great North Woods offer all the beauty of the White Mountains without the hordes of tourists and shopping outlets present in the national forest's southern reaches. The rural landscape is composed of thick pine forests, where timber companies harvest the trees that fuel the mills of Gorham and Berlin, the brick North Country mill town where this ride begins.

Berlin, once known as Maynesburgh, is still called "The City that Trees Built." By the late 19th century, the world's largest paper mills lined the banks of the Androscoggin River. When the river was swollen with a torrent of spring snowmelt, it was akin to a bustling freeway. Men working as teams of river drivers floated massive logs on a perilous journey from the lofty northern forests downstream to Gorham and Berlin's lumberyards and paper and pulp mills. These legendary drives have evolved into road trips by logging truck, but it remains rough work.

Today Berlin still revolves around its pulp mill, whose towering smokestacks form the epicenter of the city. In recent years, the relationship has become tenuous, with a dire pattern of closings and layoffs, but for now the mill is up and running. It's a working factory town, with a fine collection of historic buildings along Main

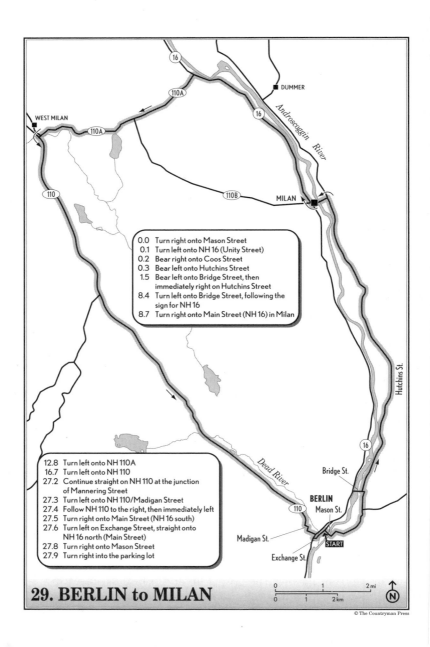

WEST MILAN

DUMMER

Androscoggin River

16

110A

110A

110

110B

MILAN

0.0 Turn right onto Mason Street
0.1 Turn left onto NH 16 (Unity Street)
0.2 Bear right onto Coos Street
0.3 Bear left onto Hutchins Street
1.5 Bear left onto Bridge Street, then
immediately right on Hutchins Street
8.4 Turn left onto Bridge Street, following the
sign for NH 16
8.7 Turn right onto Main Street (NH 16) in Milan

Hutchins St.

12.8 Turn left onto NH 110A
16.7 Turn left onto NH 110
27.2 Continue straight on NH 110 at the junction
of Mannering Street
27.3 Turn left onto NH 110/Madigan Street
27.4 Follow NH 110 to the right, then immediately left
27.5 Turn right onto Main Street (NH 16 south)
27.6 Turn left on Exchange Street, straight onto
NH 16 north (Main Street)
27.8 Turn right onto Mason Street
27.9 Turn right into the parking lot

Dead River

16

Bridge St.

BERLIN
110   Mason St.

Madigan St.

Exchange St.

START

29. BERLIN to MILAN

0   1   2 mi
0   1   2 km

N

© The Countryman Press

Street. The beauty of the surrounding forest stands in stark contrast to Berlin's brick cityscape, but they're historically and inextricably linked by the business of timber. On Main Street just north of downtown, the Northern Forest Heritage Park and Brown Pulp & Paper Company House Museum highlight Berlin's industrial history and the North Country's working forest since the 1880s. The annual Great North Woods Lumberjack Championships are held here.

You'll leave Berlin by riding past the pulp mill on a busy road that quickly becomes rural and thick with pines. (The North Country is nearly 97 percent forested.) As you ride north toward Milan, the peaks to the east are Maine's rugged Mahoosuc Range. Along the way, you'll pass Nansen Ski Club, regarded as the nation's oldest such club. It was founded in 1872, and is widely credited with bringing the sport of Nordic skiing from Sweden to America. The club maintains more than 20 miles of trails between the Androscoggin River and the Maine border.

Milan, a small farming community on the banks of the Androscoggin, has a market where you can stop for food and drinks. Many North Country residents are of French-Canadian heritage, and French is widely spoken and apparent on signs around town and on local radio stations. From the lofty heights of NH 110, enjoy the panoramic views of the impossibly huge peaks of the Presidential Range as you head back south to Berlin.

DIRECTIONS FOR THE RIDE
The ride begins at the municipal parking lot on Mason Street, behind City Hall in downtown Berlin.

0.0 From the parking area, turn right onto Mason Street.

0.1 At the traffic light, turn left onto NH 16 (Unity Street).
Here you'll pass the old railroad depot.

0.2 At the pulp mill, bear right onto Coos Street.

0.3 Bear left onto Hutchins Street.

1.5 Bear left onto Bridge Street, then immediately right to continue on

Hutchins Street.

1.6 Pass sprawling lumberyards and a neighborhood of older homes.
This is where the timber is stored before being processed downstream at the pulp mill.

3.7 Suddenly the road narrows and enters a cool pine forest.
In this stretch of woods is the Nansen Cross-Country Ski Touring Center, founded by Scandinavian immigrants in the 19th century. The center's steel-tower ski jump is the second highest in the United States. Across the road is the Nansen Wayside Park, a small picnic area on the river.

7.0 Near the Milan town line, the forest opens to wider views of farmland and the mountains far to the north.

8.4 At the small Berlin Airport, turn left onto Bridge Street, following the sign for NH 16.
Cross the Androscoggin River again to reach the tiny center of Milan.

Reflecting on a long day's ride

8.7 At the stop sign, turn right onto Main Street (NH 16) in Milan, following the sign to Errol.
There's a small grocery store with a deli at the corner. This agricultural area, with long cornfields planted along the river, stands in stark contrast to industrial Berlin.

12.8 Turn left onto NH 110A, following the signs to West Milan and Groveton.
Ride away from the river and up into the forest on this rural back road that combines some steep climbs and descents with rolling terrain.

16.7 At the stop sign, turn left to ride east on NH 110.
There's a convenience store at this junction, just outside the village of West Milan. After a pair of mile-long climbs along this road, you'll begin the descent into Berlin. The pulp mill smokestacks and the lumberyards stacked high with logs are visible on the outskirts of the city.

27.2 In Berlin, continue straight on NH 110 at the junction of Mannering Street.

27.3 Turn left onto NH 110 (Madigan Street).

27.4 Follow NH 110 as it turns right at a stop sign, then immediately left at a blinking traffic light.

27.5 At the traffic light, turn right onto Main Street (NH 16 south).

27.6 Turn left on Exchange Street; follow this short street as it leads straight onto NH 16 north (Main Street).

27.8 At the traffic light in front of City Hall, turn right onto Mason Street.

27.9 Turn right into the parking lot to end the ride.

Bicycle Shops

Moriah Sports, 101 Main Street (US 2), Gorham; 603-466-5050;
www.moriahsports.com

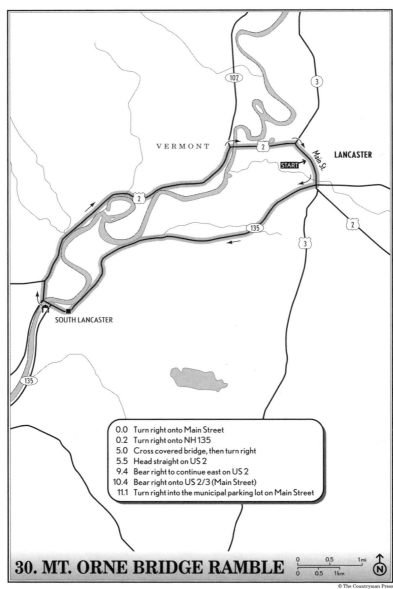

VERMONT

102

3

2   LANCASTER

START

Main St.

2

135

2

3

SOUTH LANCASTER

135

0.0 Turn right onto Main Street
0.2 Turn right onto NH 135
5.0 Cross covered bridge, then turn right
5.5 Head straight on US 2
9.4 Bear right to continue east on US 2
10.4 Bear right onto US 2/3 (Main Street)
11.1 Turn right into the municipal parking lot on Main Street

30. MT. ORNE BRIDGE RAMBLE

0   0.5   1mi
0   0.5   1km

N

Mount Orne Covered Bridge Ramble

- **DISTANCE:** 11.1 miles
- **TERRAIN:** Flat and gently rolling back roads
- **DIFFICULTY:** Easy
- **RECOMMENDED BICYCLE:** Touring/road bike or hybrid

Lancaster is the seat of Coos County, a vast area of more than a million acres stretching from the Presidential Range to the Canadian border. It has the distinction of being the state's largest county, covering most of the massive northern tip of New Hampshire. The area is more forested than any other region in New Hampshire, and it's often the first to see snow and the last to see summer. Lancaster's handsome village green is lined with shops and historic homes and churches; the outlying hills between the Connecticut and Israel Rivers are covered in a patchwork of farm fields and woodlands.

Lancaster resident and environmentally-conscious politician John Sinclair Weeks spearheaded the bill that established the White Mountain National Forest in 1911. Decades of unrestricted logging of the state's virgin forest were reducing mountain scenery to wide swaths of clear-cut land vulnerable to forest fire, erosion, and flooding. The Weeks Act set aside 768,000 acres, creating the first national forest in the country and what still stands as the largest such forest in the East. Today, the congressman's 420-acre summer estate atop Mount Prospect is open to visitors, who come to snowshoe, picnic, hike, or just enjoy the sweeping views of the

Connecticut River valley. Weeks State Park spreads across much of the 2,059-foot mountain, and includes a 1912 lodge (now a museum) and an 87-foot-high fieldstone fire tower.

A highlight of this tour is the picturesque Mount Orne Covered Bridge, which connects farmland on both sides of the Connecticut River. The 267-foot bridge has spanned the river between Lancaster and Lunenburg, Vermont, since 1911, when it was built to replace an earlier bridge that was destroyed by a logjam in 1905. The Vermont side offers spectacular views of New Hampshire's open, rolling farmland backed by the massive hulks of the mountains in the Kilkenny Wilderness Area, including Mount Cabot. Also in Lancaster is the 1862 Mechanic Street Covered Bridge, spanning the Israel River off US 2/3.

DIRECTIONS FOR THE RIDE
The ride begins in Lancaster at the municipal parking lot next to the Great North Woods Welcome Center on Main Street.

The North Country's rural landscape of farms and forest

0.0 Turn right out of the parking lot onto Main Street.
Use caution riding through this busy downtown area of shops and eateries.

0.2 At the blinking light just after the bridge, turn right onto NH 135, heading south toward Dalton.
After a short climb through a neighborhood of old homes, the road continues up past a llama farm, then flattens as it cuts through rural farmland on its way toward the Connecticut River.

5.0 Cross the Mount Orne Covered Bridge, following the sign to Lunenburg, Vermont. Once across the river, turn right to follow the riverbank north.
From here you can really appreciate the beauty of the New Hampshire mountains. The backdrop they create is majestic, especially when covered in snow, a common sight when riding in spring and fall.

5.5 At the stop sign, head straight on US 2.
This road is busy, but has a wide shoulder to ride on.

9.4 At the intersection of VT 102, bear right to continue east on US 2.
Cross the Connecticut River on a green steel bridge to return to New Hampshire.

10.4 At the junction of US 3, bear right onto US 2/3, following the sign to Lancaster.

11.1 Turn right into the municipal parking lot on Main Street to end the ride.

Bicycle Shops

Littleton Bike Shop, 87 Main Street (US 302), Littleton; 603-444-3437; www.littletonbike.com

Moriah Sports, 101 Main Street (US 2), Gorham; 603-466-5050; www.moriahsports.com

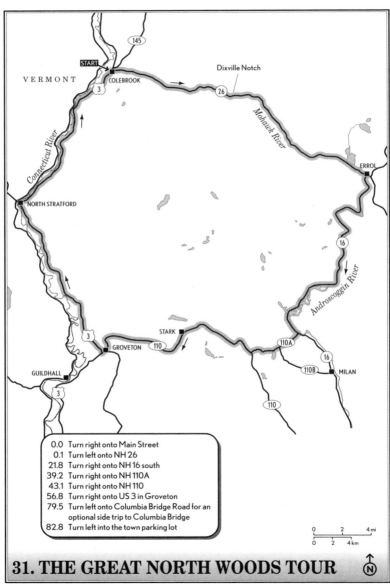

VERMONT

START

COLEBROOK

145

Dixville Notch

26

Mohawk River

ERROL

Connecticut River

NORTH STRATFORD

16

Androscoggin River

STARK

110

3

GROVETON

110A

16

GUILDHALL

110B

MILAN

3

110

0.0   Turn right onto Main Street
0.1   Turn left onto NH 26
21.8   Turn right onto NH 16 south
39.2   Turn right onto NH 110A
43.1   Turn right onto NH 110
56.8   Turn right onto US 3 in Groveton
79.5   Turn left onto Columbia Bridge Road for an
       optional side trip to Columbia Bridge
82.8   Turn left into the town parking lot

0   2   4 mi
0   2   4 km

31. THE GREAT NORTH WOODS TOUR

N

The Great North Woods Tour

- **DISTANCE:** 82.8 miles
- **TERRAIN:** Rolling hills mixed with steep climbs and descents
- **DIFFICULTY:** Very strenuous
- **RECOMMENDED BICYCLE:** Touring/road bike

North of the White Mountains is a vast wilderness that most visitors to New Hampshire never see. Many of the people who do travel to the Great North Woods, or *Grands Bois du Nord,* do so for the first-rate hunting, fishing, and snowmobiling. Some who live here—a mere 35,000 in all—still farm. Many are employed as loggers by huge timber companies. And others work in the mill towns of Berlin and Groveton to the south.

New Hampshire's narrow northern top is blanketed in massive pine forests that stand in living testimony to the timber industry that the Great North Woods supports. Thousands of acres are protected as public land, including the 40,000-acre Nash Stream Forest and nearly 800,000 acres in the White Mountain National Forest. Much of the rest is owned by lumber and paper companies, with small tracts maintained by environmental groups like The Nature Conservancy.

Naturally, wildlife abounds in these forests, from moose and bear to loons and bald eagles. If you come to this rugged, mountainous corner of the state to ride, you're all but guaranteed seclusion. More and more outdoor enthusiasts are discovering this area's pristine wilderness hiking and the canoeing and kayaking available among the inlets of Lake Umbagog, the most isolated lake in the state. This large body of water straddles the Maine border and includes a national wildlife refuge.

An estimated five thousand moose roam these northern mountains. Moose tours are rising in popularity, hauling tourists around in buses at night to glimpse New England's largest wild animal. The North Country Moose Festival and Moose Mania are annual summertime celebrations in North Country towns, with parades, street fairs, concerts, and special events throughout the region. Moose are most often seen along roadsides at dusk and dawn and around lakes and other wetlands.

The ride starts in Colebrook and cuts a wide arc through the Great North Woods, from the Connecticut River valley in the west to the Upper Androscoggin Valley along the Maine border to the east. It follows the course of four rivers—the Connecticut, Androscoggin, Mohawk, and Upper Ammonoosuc—through a beautiful landscape of thick pine forest and working dairy farms. New Hampshire's White Mountains, the Green Mountains in Vermont, and the mountain ranges of western Maine provide panoramic views.

At the turn of the last century, some 40 grand resort hotels were scattered throughout New Hampshire. Today, only four remain: three are in the White Mountains and the northernmost one is passed on this tour.

The Balsams is tucked amid 15,000 mountainous acres in Dixville Notch. The palatial hotel is a throwback to the long-ago era of New England's grand resorts, when wealthy vacationers would arrive by train and stay for weeks at a time. Dixville Notch is also famous for its role as the first community in the nation to cast ballots in presidential primaries.

Tiny Errol is a rural crossroads community of less than five hundred residents, close to the Maine border and Lake Umbagog, an expansive wetlands home to countless species of birds and mammals, including moose, otter, and bald eagles, and the source of the mighty Androscoggin. Many outfitters who lead kayaking, canoeing, and fishing trips, including New England's oldest kayaking school, use Errol as a base. Here, you'll head south to follow the river's winding course, where the pristine countryside is known as Thirteen Mile Woods. The Androscoggin Wayside Park is a pretty picnic area set on a bluff overlooking the river.

Heading back west into the high, open land between the two river valleys, you'll come across the oft-photographed village of Stark, an unexpected surprise in this high, desolate area. The prim 19th-century village is quintessential New England, complete with white clapboard inn, school, library, and church, all clustered around a covered bridge spanning the Upper Ammonoosuc River. If the charming scene looks familiar, you may have seen it on one of the many postcards and calendars it has graced over the years.

This area was the site of Camp Stark, which held German and Austrian war prisoners during World War II. It was the only such

The Union Church and Stark covered bridge were built in the 1850s along the Upper Ammonoosuc River.

camp in New Hampshire, but one of a few hundred across the country. Prisoners worked as loggers, supplying wood for the paper and lumber mills to the south, in Berlin and Groveton.

The mill town of Groveton is the last stop on this tour before the return north to Colebrook. It's dominated by the huge Wausau paper mill, but also boasts a quaint covered bridge (open to pedestrians only), a small museum in an 18th-century meetinghouse, and a really good diner. The lofty Percy Peaks provide a dramatic backdrop.

Note: This is an extremely challenging route—only experienced cyclists should try tackling it in one day. It's recommended that you stretch the ride over two days. Lodging options along the way are listed at the end of the chapter.

DIRECTIONS FOR THE RIDE

The tour begins in the center of Colebrook. Park in the town parking lot on Main Street, across from the public library. Be sure to pick up food and drinks in Colebrook; small markets are scattered along the way, but they are few and far between. There are no bike shops on this entire route—the closest shops are in Gorham and Littleton—so it's wise to carry a couple of spare tubes and tools to change a flat tire.

0.0 Turn right from the parking area onto Main Street.

0.1 At the traffic light, turn left onto NH 26, heading east toward Dixville Notch.
This high rural road—a state-designated scenic and cultural byway—follows the Mohawk River and climbs steadily toward Dixville Notch, New Hampshire's northernmost mountain pass.

11.3 Ride through Dixville Notch and prepare for the long descent out of the mountains. Use caution on the very steep descent just past Dixville Notch State Park.
The Balsams Grand Resort Hotel is a sprawling 19th-century hotel perched above Lake Gloriette and beneath Abenaki Mountain in the 15,000-acre Balsams Wilderness. There was a time—the late 1800s, to be exact—when these great resorts were all over the state. Today, The Balsams is one of only a few remaining, and the farthest north.

21.8 At the stop sign in Errol, turn right on NH 16 south.

Errol is a tiny North Country town on the Androscoggin River. There is a market here for food and supplies. Just west of the village is the river's source, the 13,000-acre Lake Umbagog National Wildlife Refuge. Bald eagles and moose are among the abundance of wildlife residing here. The road follows the river as it twists south through the pristine Thirteen Mile Woods Scenic Area, popular with canoeists and anglers.

39.2 Turn right at the junction of NH 110A, heading west toward Stark.

The road climbs and dips through the Ammonoosuc Valley, with spectacular views of the northern peaks along the way.

43.1 Turn right at the junction of NH 110, continuing west toward Stark.

50.1 Pass through the village of Stark.

The sheer walls of the Devil's Slide rise above the picture-perfect quaintness of this village named for Revolutionary War General John Stark. Past the 1853 Union Church and 134-foot covered bridge is the handsome Stark Village Inn, a rambling farmhouse on the banks of the Upper Ammonoosuc River. The 1862 covered bridge was washed downstream in the 1890s, and residents used oxen to pull it back to town for renovation.

56.8 At the stop sign, turn right on US 3 in Groveton.

Check out the 1852 covered bridge before leaving town.

79.5 Turn left onto Columbia Bridge Road for an optional side trip to Columbia Bridge.

This historic bridge, 145 feet in length, spans the Connecticut River from Columbia village to Lemington, Vermont. It's the northernmost bridge connecting the two states, built in 1912 to replace a bridge at the site that had burned down a year earlier. Notice how narrow the river is here compared with the southern reaches of the state.

82.8 In downtown Colebrook, turn left into the town parking lot to end the ride.

Bicycle Shops

Littleton Bike Shop, 87 Main Street (US 302), Littleton; 603-444-3437; www.littletonbike.com

Moriah Sports, 101 Main Street (US 2), Gorham; 603-466-5050;
www.moriahsports.com

Lodging

Stark Village Inn, Route 110 (P.O. Box 389), Stark, NH 03582; 603-636-2644

Magalloway River Inn, Route 16, Errol, NH 03579; 603-482-9883

The Balsams Grand Resort Hotel, Route 26, Dixville Notch, NH 03576; 1-800-255-0600, or in New Hampshire, 1-800-255-0800

32

Northern River Roads: Colebrook to Pittsburg

- **DISTANCE:** 39.7 miles
- **TERRAIN:** A mix of rolling hills, flat roads, and a few steep climbs
- **DIFFICULTY:** Strenuous
- **RECOMMENDED BICYCLE:** Touring/road bike

This rural northern area of New Hampshire and Vermont is alternately known as the North Country, the Great North Woods, the Connecticut Lakes, North of the Notches, and *Grands Bois du Nord*. No matter what name you use, it's a land apart, the edge of a vast semiwilderness of rugged mountains and sweeping vistas straight out of a movie set.

You'll explore the remote area between Colebrook and Pittsburg, two tiny communities just south of the Canadian border. Pittsburg is the largest New Hampshire town in terms of land—more than 300 square miles—and one of the smallest in population, as suggested by its sparse village center. Its immense forests, thick with Scotch pine and blue spruce, lend this northernmost New Hampshire town a vaguely frontier-like aura. Both towns are popular sporting centers, drawing hunters, anglers, snowmobilers, and campers from around New England and beyond.

Pittsburg's 19th century residents were known for their independent-minded and rebellious nature. Frustrated with ongoing border disputes, a group of 60 residents formed an

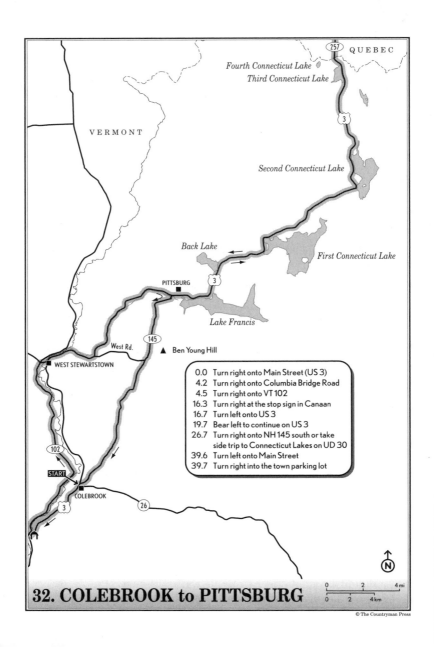

Fourth Connecticut Lake

Third Connecticut Lake

QUEBEC

VERMONT

Second Connecticut Lake

Back Lake

First Connecticut Lake

PITTSBURG

Lake Francis

West Rd.

▲ Ben Young Hill

WEST STEWARTSTOWN

0.0   Turn right onto Main Street (US 3)
4.2   Turn right onto Columbia Bridge Road
4.5   Turn right onto VT 102
16.3 Turn right at the stop sign in Canaan
16.7 Turn left onto US 3
19.7 Bear left to continue on US 3
26.7 Turn right onto NH 145 south or take
      side trip to Connecticut Lakes on UD 30
39.6 Turn left onto Main Street
39.7 Turn right into the town parking lot

START

COLEBROOK

N

0   2   4 mi
0   2   4 km

32. COLEBROOK to PITTSBURG

independent territory, the United Inhabitants of the Indian Stream Republic, and remained seceded from the United States for nearly a decade before Pittsburg was incorporated into New Hampshire. North Country residents still maintain an identity of their own, a rugged spirit that originates from a combination of history, geographic isolation, and extreme winter weather.

Pittsburg is home to the source of the New England's longest river, what the local Abenaki Indians called *Quinn-attuck-auke,* meaning the "Long Deer Place." The Connecticut River begins as a trickle at the Fourth Connecticut Lake near Quebec, the humble beginning of a mighty course—255 miles along the New Hampshire border alone—to Long Island Sound in Connecticut. An optional side trip to the river's source, past the Third, Second, and First Connecticut Lakes, is detailed below.

The tour begins in Colebrook, a small, no-frills town of several hundred residents. Main Street is the busy business and commercial center for much of the Great North Woods, as well as communities across the river in Vermont's Northeast Kingdom.

You'll cross the Connecticut River into Lemington, Vermont, on the Columbia Bridge, built in 1912 by Charles Babbitt. It is the northernmost of several covered bridges connecting the two states, and arguably one of the prettiest. Sometimes the river may be hard to see—the road snakes inland or a field of high corn blocks the view. But then around a bend, it suddenly reappears, dark and wide, and the road once again follows its meandering contours. From this vantage point, enjoy the panoramic views of northern New Hampshire's farms and forests on your way north to Pittsburg. The last stop in Vermont is Canaan, a key Civil War–era stop on the underground railroad to Canada.

Timber harvesting is the big industry in the North Woods, so it's quite possible that you may be sharing the road with logging trucks from time to time. The hills are laced with dirt logging roads, as well as lakes, streams, and sporting camps.

This is moose country, evidenced by the proliferation of road signs warning of collisions with these hefty members of the deer family, which can weigh half a ton. Moose are most active along roadways at dawn, dusk, and during the night, but you still may

194 THE GREAT NORTH WOODS

see one of the five thousand or so that reside here. The summer-time North Country Moose Festival, with its car show, parades, and moose tours, draws thousands of visitors. The side trip to the Connecticut Lakes follows a section of US 3 known locally as "Moose Alley."

Heading north on US 3 around Stewartstown you'll cross the 45th parallel, marking the halfway point between the Equator and the North Pole. You'll pass over it a second time on your return trip to Colebrook.

DIRECTIONS FOR THE RIDE

The ride begins on Main Street in Colebrook. Park in the town parking lot across from the public library.

0.0 Turn right from the parking area onto Main Street (US 3).
There is a convenience store in town where you can pick up food and drinks before you head south.

Farm fields high above the Connecticut River

1.4 Pass the Shrine of Our Lady of Grace on both sides of the road.
A statue of a carved motorcycle next to a pair of riders kneeling in prayer is a testa-ment to the thousands of bikers who make the pilgrimage here.

4.2 Turn right onto Columbia Bridge Road to cross the Connecticut River on the Columbia Bridge, following the sign for VT 102.
This 145-foot-long covered bridge from Columbia village to Lemington, Vermont, was built in 1912 to replace a bridge at the site that had burned down a year earlier. The river flows smoothly underneath, significantly narrower than in the southern reaches of the state.

4.5 At the stop sign, turn right onto VT 102.
Pedal through pristine farmland that slopes to the riverbank. On this side, Vermont's Mount Monadnock soars overhead at 3,140 feet. Enjoy the wide-open pastoral views from this rolling country road dotted with farmhouses in various stages of repair, from meticulously restored to literally falling down.

8.5 At the junction of VT 26, continue straight.
The farther north you ride, the better the scenery gets. The road, getting narrower by the mile, is often muddied by tractors and cattle crossing over from fields to barns.

16.3 Turn right at the stop sign in Canaan, following the signs for Colebrook and West Stewartstown, New Hampshire, and US 3.
There are a couple of diners on the Vermont side of the Connecticut River and a small market across the bridge in New Hampshire.

16.7 At the blinking traffic light in West Stewartstown, turn left onto US 3, fol-lowing the sign to Pittsburg.
After making the short, steep climb out of town, you'll pass the roadside marker designating the 45th parallel, the line of latitude marking the halfway point between the North Pole and the Equator.

18.0 At the sign for U.S. Customs and VT 253, continue north on US 3.

19.7 At the Clarksville Store, bear left to continue on US 3 (West Road goes to the right).

26.7 In the center of Pittsburg, turn right onto NH 145 south. (Side trip to the Connecticut Lakes: Stay on US 3 north for about 22 miles to reach the Fourth Connecticut Lake. You'll pass by all four of the Connecticut Lakes, strung like jewels along small streams that eventually form the Connecticut River. A half-mile hiking trail at the U.S. Customs station leads to the official source.)

This high country road climbs to the top of Ben Young Hill on the route's most challenging ascent, but the panoramic views of the White Mountains and rolling farmland—not to mention the descent to Colebrook—are well worth it.

29.5 Reach the top of Ben Young Hill.
Use caution descending this narrow road.

31.0 Cross back over the 45th parallel.

37.3 Pass Beaver Brook Falls and its picnic area.

39.6 At the stop sign in Colebrook, turn left onto Main Street and cross the bridge.

39.7 Turn right into the town parking lot to end the ride.

Bicycle Shops

Littleton Bike Shop, 87 Main Street (US 302), Littleton; 603-444-3437; www.littletonbike.com

Moriah Sports, 101 Main Street (US 2), Gorham; 603-466-5050; www.moriahsports.com